NULLIFICATION
THE CASE FOR DECENTRALIZING THE FEDERAL GOVERNMENT

by Frank Salvato

DEDICATION

To Cj...the love I have searched for my entire life and finally found. In dedication to your steadfast belief in me, my dreams, and my abilities; and for your unwavering love of country, liberty, and freedom.

To my Mother...who nurtured critical thinking skills in her children and who helped me to successfully navigate the perilous seas of the political realm.

To my sister, Frances... whose kind heart and true soul always helped to keep me balanced in life.

To my dear departed friend Nick...who taught me how to cherish the now and to keep the moment in your heart forever.

CONTENTS

ABSTRACT: SUMMARY

"The powers delegated by the proposed Constitution to the federal government are few and defined. Those which are to remain in the State governments are numerous and indefinite."

— James Madison

There can be no doubt that neo-fascistic socialism is on the move in the United States today. Those who value the importance of history understand that fascism's introduction into our culture isn't a new development. The genesis of what Mark Levin has identified as *American Marxism*[1] and before him what Jonah Goldberg labeled *Liberal Fascism*[2], exploded onto the scene at the turn of the 20th Century. It was ushered into the circles of government during Woodrow Wilson's administration, was significantly advanced during Franklin D. Roosevelt's administration, cemented itself into our governmental permaculture during the Johnson administration, and has encroached into our society steadily and incrementally ever since, exploding into social dominance during the Obama and Biden administrations.

Unknown to many is the fact that famous – or infamous – fascists of the Wilsonian Era were in awe of the type of fascism the Wilson administration brought to the American government. Italy's Mussolini went so far as to pen newspaper columns congratulating both Wilson and Roosevelt on implementing such potent fascism into American society. The admiration was reciprocal with Roosevelt, pre-World War II, who stated that he found Mussolini "an admirable Italian gentleman."[3]

When the Framers created the Republic – through the codification of the US Constitution and soon after in the Bill of Rights, they did so with the purpose of putting the

---

[1] https://amzn.to/42og2H5

[2] https://amzn.to/3oRB8zR

[3] https://dailycaller.com/2016/12/13/fdr-praised-mussolini-and-loved-fascism/_

newly created government on notice that its powers had limitations and boundaries; that it was not the lord of the people, rather the people were the lords of government.

To that end, the tenets and principles that were enshrined in the Constitution and the Bill of Rights – among them the rights to free speech, the free practice of religion, the unfettered redress of government, the right to bear arms, the right to be secure in our persons and possessions, among the other enumerated and inalienable rights, were assumed to be an omnipresent constant in our society; that we, as a people, lived those rights every second of every day as a natural state.

But getting 250 years on, our rights cannot be so assumed. The federal government has transgressed the limitations enumerated in the Constitution and the Bill of Rights and has incrementally co-opted power to a point where the sovereign rights of the people and the individual states have been significantly eroded. In its current form, the United States federal government is operating with no boundaries, no checks or balances; it is operating in a neo-fascist and despotic manner, utilizing an unelected bureaucracy – what many call the "Deep State" – to circumvent the true representation of the sovereign people.

Under the Wilson administration (coincidentally the exact moment the influence of the Frankfurt School[4] took root

____

[4]

https://www.americanthinker.com/articles/2018/01/the_frankfurt_school_and_c
ultural_marxism.html

in the United States), we lost the basic protections that were built into our Republic. While the US House of Representatives was meant to be the chamber in which the direct representation of the people was executed at the federal level, the US Senate was supposed to be the chamber where each of the 50 states was represented; where the rights and sovereignty of the states were protected.

In the Constitution's original form, each state's legislature was empowered to choose two senators to represent their state:

> *"The Senate of the United States shall be composed of two Senators from each State, **chosen by the Legislature thereof**, for six Years; and each Senator shall have one Vote."*[5]

But the 17th Amendment changed that, destroying the balance the Framers crafted in our Founding Documents:

> *"The Senate of the United States shall be composed of two Senators from each State, **elected by the people thereof**, for six years; and each Senator shall have one vote."*[6]

With the passage of the 17th Amendment, the nation, as our Framers and Founders bequeathed to us, ended; it exists no more. The states, with that vote, were left

---

[5] https://www.archives.gov/founding-docs/constitution-transcript#1-3

[6] https://www.archives.gov/founding-docs/amendments-11-27#xvii

unprotected from the manipulation of open politicization and the overreach of a politicized federal government; an overreach that has subjugated the states to the will of a federal government whose fidelity to its electorate is in decline to the point of being tantamount to non-existent.

The protection and adequate representation of the sovereign fifty states was the *sole purpose* for the appointments of US Senators by the state legislatures. They were emissaries to the federal government *from* the states, charged with safeguarding the sovereignty of the states they were sent to represent.

In the original configuration – the constitutional configuration, the people were represented, the states were represented, and the laws of the land emerging from those two chambers centered on the sovereignty of both the people *and* the states; the federal government's Executive Branch tasked with executing those laws with fidelity and within the limitations outlined in the Constitution and Bill of Rights to include the 10th Amendment.

With the 17th Amendment, which allowed for the direct election of senators by the people, the protections afforded the states were eliminated, creating an upper chamber similar to the lower chamber; a second chamber vulnerable to the divisive poison of national politics, of which President Washington warned in his Farewell Address[7]. At the moment the 17th Amendment became

---

[7]

https://www.senate.gov/artandhistory/history/resources/pdf/Washingtons_Fare

law, the states became subservient to the federal government.

And because protection for the sovereignty of states no longer existed – given that the US Senate was transformed into an over-glorified US House of Representatives, the politicization of the whole of the Legislative Branch had been completed, making it easier for well-funded activist groups and ideologues – like Marxists and fascists in *all* their forms to include today's globalists – to advocate for laws that serve special interests over the "common good," progressively deteriorating our rights as citizens of sovereign states and as individuals; through laws that move the United States toward neo-fascistic socialism – and then communism – under the authority of global governance.

Another constitutional failure that took place initially, again under the Wilson administration and significantly advanced under the Roosevelt administration, was the bureaucratization of the federal government.[8]

Instead of the Legislative Branch creating accurate, well-written, and *complete* pieces of legislation, the politicized bodies of that branch began producing generalized pieces of legislation, leaving the crafting of the details in said legislation to the Executive Branch departments, agencies, and commissions. This practice is detrimental to the country for two reasons.

---

well_Address.pdf

[8] https://nationalaffairs.com/storage/app/uploads/public/58e/1a4/bfb/ 58e1a4bfb0f58240877944.pdf

First, it allocates legislative power to the Executive Branch in allowing its departments, agencies, and commissions to define the parameters of legislation, traversing the Separation of Powers. This, in and of itself, is unconstitutional.

Second, it allows the Executive Branch to act unilaterally upon the states and the people via regulation and mandate, again, something that is unconstitutional. A perfect example comes to us in the 2020 COVID pandemic which delivered to the people federal health mandates to include the domain of the total of the private sector without the necessary legislation to give those mandates the force of law.

During the 2020 COVID pandemic, the Biden administration made no secret of its aggressive coercion of the private sector, using the Occupational Safety & Health Administration (OSHA) to apply regulation as a force of law to strong-arm corporations and small business entities into compliance with Executive Branch mandates.[9]

This type of authoritarian cancer – something that our Framers most likely would have gone to war to prevent and/or overthrow, has increasingly crept into the private sector; into whole industries that engage in "woke" social engineering behavior that marginalizes the rights of individuals and which attempts to punish state

---

[9] https://www.npr.org/2021/11/04/1048939858/osha-biden-vaccine-mandate-employers-100-workers

governments. Perfect examples of this come in Major League Baseball's move out of Georgia for the 2021 All-Star Game[10] and the Federal Reserve Bank and Wall Street's embrace of ESG scoring.[11]

All of this culminates in the facilitation of the advancement of neo-fascistic socialism in our federal government, enjoining our corporations into public-private partnerships reminiscent of the cooperative partnerships[12] that were prevalent in Mussolini's Italy; a neo-fascism that bleeds into the full fabric of our society.

The pathway back to constitutionalism rests in the restoration of state sovereignty as it was secured in the original Founding Documents. The roadmap leads to a destination that is a balanced anti-federalism.

To briefly touch on anti-federalism – which will be addressed more fully in a later chapter, the anti-federalist position was cultivated during the Constitutional Convention in response to serious concerns about the creation and implementation of a powerful central government. Chief among the concerns of those seated at the convention – concerns that have come to fruition today – was that an all-powerful centralized federal

---

[10] https://www.espn.com/mlb/story/_/id/31183822/mlb-moving-all-star-game-atlanta-georgia-voting-law

[11] https://www.bloomberg.com/news/articles/2021-12-31/how-blackrock-s-invisible-hand-helped-make-esg-a-hot-ticket#xj4y7vzkg

[12] https://www.cato.org/commentary/economic-leadership-secrets-benito-mussolini

government would encroach on the freedom of individuals and undermine state sovereignty.

So, state governments that still believe government serves the people and not the other way around, must engage in three efforts to lead the nation back to health:

- The embrace and utilization of nullification
- The pro-active elimination of the federal government's ability to inflict retributive pain
- A constitutional re-codification of limitations on the federal government

The federal government can only exact retributive pain on the states through the withholding of federal tax dollars; tax dollars derived, ironically, from the citizens of the sovereign states. For the states to effectively eliminate the federal government's vehicle for the financial coercion of the states, state governments might set themselves to crafting laws that disrupt the direct extraction or remittance of federal tax dollars from a state's citizenry – perhaps requiring that those dollars pass through the state governments for remittance in bulk and at one time.

It would be in the aftermath of codifying such legislation – to neuter the ability of the federal government to exact retributive pain against a non-conformist state, that the vehicle of nullification could be fully employed against every unfunded federal mandate and every federal act that is counter to the Bill of Rights and the US Constitution.

Acknowledging that the people of the United States exist in a constant "State of Rights" is integral to empowering the state governments to stand up to the tyranny of the minority in what is today's non-representative federal government.

It will be a long road and not without its own cooperative difficulties. But with many state governors awakening to the fact that the federal government is out of control and on the cusp of totalitarianism, there is hope that the gubernatorial leaders of the fifty sovereign states will counter the embrace of the Marxist-promoting neo-fascism that currently holds our federal government hostage.

THE DANGERS OF CENTRALIZED GOVERNMENT

"The powers of the federal government are enumerated; it can only operate in certain cases; it has legislative powers on defined and limited objects, beyond which it cannot extend its jurisdiction."

– James Madison

While centralized government structures – such as the one that has evolved here in the United States – have been prevalent throughout history, they are not without inherent dangers; dangers that pose direct threats to representative government, constitutional democracy, state sovereignty, and individual liberty.

Some of the dangers associated with centralized government include the concentration of power, erosion of democratic principles, violation of human rights, lack of accountability, and the potential for increased authoritarianism. By contrast, a balanced and decentralized approach to governance safeguards the rights and liberties of individuals.

Centralized government refers to a system in which power and decision-making authority are concentrated in a single central authority, usually at the national level. At the genesis of our Republic, the Founders and Framers fully understood the dangers of centralized government. They had just executed a revolutionary war to free the thirteen colonies from the British monarch, King George III, who by virtue of his existence was the ultimate form of centralized government. What the Framers wanted to avoid was forming a government that created the temptation to devolve into one of centralized authority; they wanted to avoid creating a government over the sovereign thirteen colonies with the ability to dictate policies, create laws, and control various aspects of public life a the national level when that authority, in their views, were reserved for the individual and sovereign states. While a more centralized structure may have appeared efficient to some in theory, its dangers were evident, leading the Framers to create a system with checks and balances.

One of the primary dangers of centralized government comes to us in the concentration of power in the hands of a few individuals or a single governing entity. When power becomes centralized, it opens the door to inevitable abuses and corruption. Decision-making becomes limited to a select and elite few, reducing constitutionally prescribed representation, directly attacking the sovereignty of the individual states, and disenfranchising the citizenry from participation in the governance process. This concentration of power undermines the democratic ideals of equal opportunity for all and fair representation.

Today, we are witnessing some of the dangers being discussed occurring in our federal government. Not only are we seeing a consolidation of power – facilitated by the oligarchic political parties (of which, again, George Washington warned in his Farewell Address) – into the hands of the few, we are witnessing the undermining of democratic principles such as the checks and balances, separation of powers, and the rule of law. And as power becomes even more consolidated into both the halls of government and the depths of the federal bureaucracy, the ability of independent institutions and branches of government to act as checks on each other is disappearing, even as the apparatus consolidates to advance its own agenda separate from serving the people. This erosion of democratic principles and political morality degrades the system's ability to protect citizens from government overreach and abuse of power.

Centralized governments can pose a significant threat to human rights and civil liberties. When power is concentrated, it becomes easier for the government to suppress dissent, control information, and curtail individual freedoms. History has shown that centralized governments have been responsible for gross human rights violations, including censorship, surveillance, and persecution of political dissidents.

In our contemporary United States, we are witnessing each point mentioned above. The COVID pandemic, the political protests of January 6, 2021, and the public topics of cryptocurrency, and racial and gender identity issues have seen both the suppression of dissent and the control of information (or the battle against "misinformation", a direct attack on our First Amendment right to Freedom of Speech and the Redress of Government) to include overt censorship, an open display of government surveillance of its people and jaded, politically motivated, and oppressive persecution of political dissidents.

Another danger associated with centralized government is the complete lack of accountability. When decision-making authority rests primarily with a central authority – and especially one in which the representative Legislative Branch has unconstitutionally bequeathed its legislative authority to the regulatory bureaucratic apparatus, it becomes challenging for citizens to hold that authority accountable for any of its actions. Transparency and responsiveness suffer, leading to a culture of impunity where those in power can act without fear of consequences. This lack of accountability undermines the trust between the government and its citizens.

A perfect example of this comes in the political weaponization of the US Department of Justice, the Federal Bureau of Investigation, and the Internal Revenue Service. At no time in our nation's history has the federal government been weaponized to serve the opportunistic agendas of the political parties and, more alarmingly, the political aspirations of the Executive, than it has today. Not only are these institutions being weaponized for political purposes, the Executive Branch and the bureaucracy that serves it, tantamount to ignore the constitutionally mandated oversight of the Legislative Branch when it actually *does* execute that responsibility. The very fact that a never ending parade of Executive Branch officials must be threatened with Contempt of Congress charges for their lack of transparency proves this point.

But, perhaps the most significant danger of centralized government is the potential for authoritarianism to take hold. When power is concentrated in the hands of a single entity or a few individuals – or, in the case of the US federal government, collusive Legislative and Executive Branches, there is an increased risk of that power being abused and transformed into an oppressive regime. The absence of checks and balances, coupled with the erosion of democratic principles, creates an environment where authoritarian tendencies can thrive, resulting in the suppression of dissent and the stifling of the sovereignty of the states and individual freedoms.

History provides numerous examples of the dangers associated with centralized government. The rise of totalitarian regimes in the 20th century, such as in Nazi Germany, the Soviet Union, and the People's Republic of China (Communist China) highlights the catastrophic consequences of unchecked centralized power. The Nazis and the Soviets violated human rights, suppressed dissent, caused immense suffering, and committed sickening acts of mass genocide all due to the concentration of power in the hands of a few. In Communist China's case, these atrocities continue to this day.

Contemporary cases in various parts of the developing world, such as the erosion of democracy into oppressive socialist and then communist governments in certain countries[13], i.e. Venezuela, Nicaragua, Bolivia, and to a lesser but just as disturbing extent Canada, serve as reminders of the ongoing dangers of centralized government. The deterioration of democratic institutions, erosion of civil liberties, and the rise of populism in various parts of the world underscore the importance of a vigilant defense against the threats posed by centralized power.

---

[13] https://www.lorecentral.org/2018/11/15-examples-of-socialist-countries.html

To counteract the dangers of centralized government, a balanced and decentralized approach to governance is crucial. This balance and decentralized approach was the original form of government created for our nation. We not only had potent checks and balances, the US Constitution provided clear mandates for the limitations of the federal government's powers. Additionally, our Republic had a truly free press that held government to account while speaking truth to power; perhaps the most important check on our federal government.

But since the 17th Amendment and the expansion of the federal government's bureaucratic state during the Wilson, Roosevelt, Johnson, Bush, Obama, and Biden administrations – and the corruption of the mainstream media complex to a seat of power within the federal government apparatus, any real system of checks and balances has been rendered obsolete.

The decentralization of our federal government would disperse power and decision-making authority to various levels and branches of government – laying heavily on returning said authority and sovereignty to the now fifty states, to ensure that the federal government ceases to exist with an unchecked control of power. The decentralization of the federal government by re-empowering the fifty states to their rightful, constitutionally mandated authorities will promote inclusivity, accountability, and transparency, while protecting individual liberties and fostering a sense of governmental ownership among citizens.

The dangers posed by the current centralized US federal government are real and significant. The concentration of power (achieved), erosion of democratic principles (achieved), violation of human rights (achieved), lack of accountability (achieved and ongoing), and the progression to authoritarianism (ongoing) all underscore the need for a return to a constitutional, balanced, and decentralized approach to governance.

It is imperative to recognize, address, and eliminate these dangers from our current system of government at the federal level so that we can assure the protection of the fundamental rights and liberties of the citizenry, ensure the vitality of our Republic's democratic system, and foster a just and prosperous society.

THE SIGNIFICANCE OF THE FEDERALIST-ANTIFEDERALIST DEBATE

"And I see the danger in either case will arise principally from the conduct and views of two very unprincipled parties in the United States-two fires, between which the honest and substantial people have long found themselves situated."

— Richard Henry Lee

NULLIFICATION

The publicly held debate between those who desired a centralized government for the United States and those who understood the importance of a limited federal government culminated in the Federalist[14] and Anti-federalist Papers[15]. This very public debate holds a significant place in American history. The correspondences are accepted by historians as influential documents that played a pivotal role in the formation and interpretation of the United States Constitution.

Authored by key figures during the late 18th century, these papers represent the passionate debate surrounding the structure and powers of the federal government. This brief overview of both the Federalist and Anti-federalist Papers (whole college courses are devoted to the topics) highlights their main arguments, historical context, and enduring impact on American governance.

To understand the Federalist and Anti-federalist Papers, it is crucial to delve into the historical context in which they emerged. Following the American Revolutionary War, the fledgling United States faced a multitude of challenges, including economic instability, internal conflicts – both of a political and societal nature, and a weak central government under the Articles of Confederation.[16] Concerns quickly manifested regarding

[14] https://constitution.org/1-Constitution/fed/federa00.htm

[15] https://www.thefederalistpapers.org/wp-content/uploads/2012/11/The-Anti-Federalist-Papers-Special-Edition.pdf

[16] https://www.archives.gov/milestone-documents/articles-of-confederation#transcript

the effectiveness of the existing system, leading to calls for a stronger national (read: federal) government.

The Federalist Papers emerged as a collection of 85 essays published between 1787 and 1788. They were authored, primarily, by Alexander Hamilton, James Madison, and John Jay, who penned their contributions collectively under the pseudonym "Publius." The primary objective of these essays was to advocate for the ratification of the proposed United States Constitution.

The essays argued for the establishment of a strong and far-reaching central government, defending the necessity of a federal system and addressing concerns raised by opponents. Key issues explored in these essays included the separation of powers, the importance of an authoritative Executive Branch, the advantages of a larger Republic, and the need for a federal judiciary.

Indeed, the Federalist Papers succeeded in exerting a substantial influence on the ratification process, helping shape public opinion in favor of the proposed Constitution. Today, many continue to turn to them as an invaluable resource for interpreting the intentions of the Framers and understanding the principles underlying the American political system.

Somewhat conversely, the Anti-federalist Papers were a collection of essays written by various authors who *opposed* the ratification of a Constitution that would create an all-powerful centralized form of government for our nation. Prominent anti-federalists included Thomas

Jefferson, Patrick Henry, and George Mason, who many give equal credit for the crafting of our US Constitution. These essays, published under the collective pseudonym "Brutus," provided a counter-argument to the federalist perspective, raising concerns about the concentration of power in a central government and the potential erosion of individual liberties.

The Anti-federalist Papers challenged the proposed Constitution on multiple fronts. They voiced concerns over the lack of a Bill of Rights, the potential for the development of a tyrannical centralized government, the absence of direct representation, and the potential dominance of the governmental process by wealthy elites. The anti-federalists also advocated for a more *decentralized* system, emphasizing the importance of state sovereignty and local control.

Although the anti-federalists did not succeed in preventing the ratification of the Constitution, their arguments had a profound impact on the early years of the American Republic. Their concerns led to the adoption of the Bill of Rights; ten points that limited the authority of the newly-formed federal government while also securing individual liberties and addressing some of the anti-federalists' fears.

Furthermore, the concerns brought forth by the anti-federalists facilitated the ideological lines that were developing in our new nation via the formation of political parties and the ongoing debate surrounding federalism in the United States. Today, many recognize the anti-federalist proponents as those who champion "states' rights."

The Federalist and Anti-federalist Papers left a lasting legacy in US political and constitutional history. These public debates and arguments not only influenced the ratification of the US Constitution but also shaped subsequent interpretations of its meaning. Both sides contributed to the ongoing dialogue regarding the balance of power between the federal government and the states, as well as the protection of individual rights.

The Federalist and Anti-federalist Papers represent two distinct perspectives on the proposed United States Constitution. The federalists argued for a strong central government, with the anti-federalists expressing concerns about the potential for tyranny and the erosion of individual liberties.

The ideas and principles put forth by *both* sides continue to resonate in modern discussions about federalism, individual rights, and the proper role of government. By studying these historical documents, we gain valuable insights into the intentions of the Founding Fathers and Framers and the foundations upon which the United States was built.

NULLIFICATION

A CURSORY UNDERSTANDING OF NULLIFICATION

"A nullification is the rightful remedy whenever the government violates the Constitution."

– Thomas Jefferson

Nullification is the doctrine that empowers individual and sovereign states to invalidate what can be argued as overreaching and unconstitutional federal laws. This doctrine has played a significant role in American history and continues to do so today. From its origins in the late 18th century to its controversial applications in the 19th and 20th centuries, nullification has sparked intense debates about the balance of power between the federal government and the sovereign power of the states.

This chapter explores the historical evolution of nullification, examining key events such as the Kentucky and Virginia Resolutions, the Nullification Crisis of 1832, and the modern interpretation of nullification.[17] By analyzing these pivotal moments, we gain a deeper understanding of the constitutional tensions surrounding nullification and its lasting and ongoing impact on American governance.

The concept of nullification, the idea that states possess the power to invalidate federal laws, has been a subject of heated debate throughout American history. From its inception during the early days of the Republic to its controversial applications in more contemporary times, nullification has shaped the understanding of federalism and the balance of power between the federal government and the states.

The seeds of nullification were sown during the contentious debates over the ratification of the United

[17] https://tenthamendmentcenter.com/nullification-overview/

States Constitution. Federalists argued for a robust and authoritarian central government, while anti-federalists championed state sovereignty. These early divisions set the stage for the future and ongoing nullification controversy.

In response to the Alien and Sedition Acts of 1798, Thomas Jefferson and James Madison drafted the Kentucky and Virginia Resolutions, which articulated the theory of nullification. These resolutions claimed that states had the power to declare federal laws unconstitutional and unenforceable within their borders when their respective state legislatures codified the unconstitutionality of federal law under the 9th[18] and 10th[19] Amendments to the US Constitution in the Bill of Rights, which read, respectively:

> *"The enumeration in the Constitution, of certain rights, shall not be construed to deny or disparage others retained by the people."*

And,

> *"The powers not delegated to the United States by the Constitution, nor prohibited by it to the States, are reserved to the States respectively, or to the people."*

[18] https://www.archives.gov/founding-docs/bill-of-rights-transcript#toc-amendment-ix
[19] https://www.archives.gov/founding-docs/bill-of-rights-transcript#toc-amendment-x

In 1832, the Nullification Crisis[20] emerged as a result of escalating economic tensions between the North and South. This economic inequity would later be seen as one of the primary reasons – along with the practice and expansion of slavery – for the secession of Southern states; secession that led to the US Civil War. The Nullification Crisis was fueled by protective tariffs enacted by the federal government that placed what many in the South proclaimed to be an unfair tax burden on their states, leading to calls for nullification.

John C. Calhoun, Vice President under Andrew Jackson, championed the theory of nullification and South Carolina's right to declare federal laws void. Calhoun's exposition of nullification outlined a doctrine of state interposition against perceived federal overreach, again, under the 9th and 10th Amendments in the Bill of Rights.

President Andrew Jackson vigorously opposed nullification and took decisive action against South Carolina. His firm stance unilaterally assumed and inferred the supremacy of federal law and set an unlegislated precedent for the federal government's response to state nullification attempts.

The issues of slavery and states' rights became intrinsically linked, leading to intensified debates over nullification. Proponents of nullification argued that states had the right to protect their individual, sovereign institutions, while opponents viewed the idea of a state's

[20] https://www.khanacademy.org/humanities/us-history/the-early-republic/age-of-jackson/a/the-nullification-crisis

sovereignty and individualism as threats to the stability of the Union; as direct threats to the authoritative centralized government, which was growing more intrusive into the sovereignty of the states' by the year.

In the 1850s, South Carolina once again asserted its right to nullify federal laws, this time in response to the Fugitive Slave Act.[21] However, this attempt failed when the federal government's heavy hand of authoritarianism forced the questionable constitutional principle of federal supremacy.

The Supremacy Clause[22] in The United States Constitution has also been a central point of contention in nullification debates. The clause establishes the federal government's authority over state laws, undermining the argument for nullification as a legitimate constitutional doctrine. Those who understand the fragile balance between federalism and anti-federalism and the symbiosis required to maintain that balance recognize the Supremacy Clause as deeply flawed in its granting of what many see to be totalitarian power that compromises the rights and sovereignty of states.

In recent years, nullification has experienced a revival among both conservatives and liberals, with those on both sides of the political aisle advocating for state sovereignty and limited federal power, albeit from polar opposite vantage points. This resurgence reflects

[21] https://www.battlefields.org/learn/primary-sources/fugitive-slave-act

[22] https://www.archives.gov/founding-docs/constitution-transcript#6

broader debates over the proper scope of government authority and the limitations of that authority.

Nullification efforts have been witnessed in various policy areas, such as immigration, gun control, marijuana legalization, and the subjects of critical race theory and gender identity in school curricula. However, legal challenges and conflicting court rulings have complicated the practical implementation of nullification in modern times.

A perfect example of both a precedent for the use of nullification and a subject on which both sides have exercised nullification comes to us in the immigration/border issue. While the liberal faction has evoked the nullification of federal law at the state level by declaring the existence of sanctuary states, counties, and cities, the conservative faction advocates for the use of nullification of federal law to control illegal immigration and execute border security at the state level.[23] [24]

Another example comes to us in the vigorous debate over the activist-based teachings on the subjects of racism (and especially as it pertains to critical race theory) and gender identity in our Republic's classrooms has, again, found an embrace of nullification and states' sovereignty from factions on both ideological sides of that argument. While some states have created legislation

[23] https://www.fairus.org/issue/sanctuary-policies/do-you-live-1-11-sanctuary-states
[24] https://www.texastribune.org/2022/07/07/texas-greg-abbott-state-police-border/

that champions the inclusion of the questionable narratives surrounding both subjects in school curriculum – even in defiance of a parents authority to object to such teachings, other states have codified laws rallying to the defense of parental rights and a parent's right to have a potent voice in the education of their children.

Generally, opponents of nullification argue that it violates the Supremacy Clause and undermines the fundamental structure of the Constitution. Yet, as with the issue of sanctuary locations nullifying federal laws on immigration enforcement, they are selectively applying their ideological outrage over nullification to only those subjects that do not serve to advance their idealistic brand.

Supporters of the use of nullification and state sovereignty consistently point to the fact that state sovereignty and the limitations of the authority of the federal government are included in the Constitution and the Bill of Rights and that the 9th and 10th Amendments supersede the Supremacy Clause less the explicitly enumerated powers to the federal government in the Constitution.

Nullification has been an ongoing and recurring theme throughout US History, reflecting the ongoing tension between those who read the constitutionality of state sovereignty and the limitations of federal power in the US Constitution, and those who champion an all-powerful centralized government.

As the United States continues to grapple with questions of federalism and the balance of power, the legacy of nullification serves not only as a reminder of the enduring debates that have shaped the nation's constitutional fabric but also the role of nullification in maintaining freedom in our Republic.

THE PROBLEMS:
THE IRRECONCILABLE DIVIDE

"There is nothing which I dread so much as a division of the republic into two great parties, each arranged under its leader, and concerting measures in opposition to each other. This, in my humble apprehension, is to be dreaded as the greatest political evil under our Constitution."

– John Adams

We are a nation that exists almost terminally divided, perhaps equal to or more so than in the run-up to the US Civil War. Then, the cause of the divide was the irreconcilable issue of slavery, the expansion of slavery, and balancing the power of the federal government with the constitutionally reserved powers left to the individual states.

In the end, the cost of driving the Union to a place where a "healing of the divide" could begin was exacted in over 620,000 Americans killed and another almost 500,000 maimed or injured. Among those dead, we must count one President of the United States.[25]

Today, the divide among the people of the United States – while equal in its intensity and severity – is one based on ideology. It is a wide-ranging disagreement that finds the end-pieces of the ideological camps at polar opposites in their beliefs, while they superimpose those differences on almost every commonly held aspect of our lives.

The divide is multi-faceted and based on an array of subjects that extend from the federal government's authority in our lives to the definitions of what racism and gender are to the very definition and history of Americanism.

[25] https://www.battlefields.org/learn/articles/civil-war-casualties

The overarching questions emerging from intellectual corners – and questions that grow stronger with each ratchet of tension in the expanding divide are these:

- Is there any scenario where the current divide does not result in the fracture of the Union?

- If or when that fracture arrives, what will it look like?

- Can the Union emerge from this threat to the continuation of our Great American Experiment stronger and in a better position to thrive?

There are as many answers to those questions as there are people who ask them. But, put succinctly, there *can* be a positive resolution to each of the aforementioned questions, and the singular ingredient in the effect of those solutions is centered around the restoration of the purview of the states as the primary presence of government in each American life, with the federal government's power and purview being relegated to a literal reading of the United States Constitution.

An innovative, well-thought-out, but shockingly bold approach must be undertaken that up-ends the current relationship between the federal government and the governments of the fifty states. This approach uses the weapons of economics and nullification, rather than the weapons of war.

In the end, just as at the end of the US Civil War, we can arrive at a place where the divided American people can begin to heal; a place where the intensity and the power of the divide serve not to destroy but to rejuvenate the idea of a true Union of states, where the government most present in the lives of Americans is the government *closest* to the sovereign populations and, thus, the government most easily altered during times of bad behavior by the elected class.

We can save the Union, but to do so the fifty states must claw back their authority to rule – an authority codified in the US Constitution – from an overreaching federal government.

PROBLEM NO. 1 | A GOVERNMENT-POLITICAL CLASS THAT FEEDS OFF A DIVIDE

As has been evident over the last several General Election cycles, the elected class – and especially those who exist on the Left side of the aisle, as it is perceived – has found an exploitative tactic born of Machiavelli in "divide and rule" or "divide and conquer." [26]

This tactic has, throughout history, served to empower rulers and oligarchs to governance; to totalitarian control of populations and factions of different interests. These demographics, who collectively might be able to oppose a monarch or government's rule, are then controlled by

---

[26] https://amzn.to/42pX96T

pitting them against one another, fomenting chaos and facilitating an opportunity *for* control.

Today, this tactic is employed under the moniker "identity politics."

The American people have been manipulated into dividing themselves into demographics to be preyed upon by opportunists thirsty for power; demographics broken down into race, gender, economic status, religion, etc. Unscrupulous politicians then mold their narratives to amass a majority of voters by creating issue platforms that cobble together enough demographics to gain office; to achieve that all important 51 percent.

Almost immediately, an overwhelming number of those elected to office – not all, but most – either jettison their constituencies in favor of party politics or get swallowed up in the business of government that oozes off of K Street. In either scenario, the American people are not served.

Exploiting people emotionally to herd them into factions – some naturally occurring and others manufactured – has delivered the nation to a time and place where the populace is subservient to the government, the total opposite of what the Framers constructed.

In fact, because the elected class – what we should call the professional elected class – is dominant over a submissive population, we have regressed to the general reason for which the Framers decoupled the 13 colonies from Britain in 1776: The denial of freedom.

Today, the American people are subservient to a government steeped in special interest ideology, which has amassed an irreconcilable debt from expenditures wholly unauthorized by their constitutional purview.

The idea of the "common good", exploited by the egregious Supreme Court rulings expanding the federal government's power through the Commerce[27] and Supremacy Clauses, has exploded into micro-targeted special interest spending that only serves small swaths of the population even as it gives cover for opportunistically spendthrift policies both in foreign lands – poorly justified in the idea of alliance – and domestically in breadcrumb bribery for re-election votes.

In almost every instance of spending by the federal government, the common good, as intended at the genesis of our nation, is *not* being served. Instead, taxpayer dollars are extracted by the unprincipled professional political class, who have found their way to elected office through the tactic of "divide and rule," to grant favor to the privileged few as they enrich themselves in questionable manners all while feigning fidelity to the people and the US Constitution.

The American people are *not* being served by our government.

---

[27] https://www.law.cornell.edu/wex/commerce_clause

PROBLEM NO. 2 | AN INTRUSIVE & OVER-REACHING GOVERNMENT

Our federal government, facilitated by the problems outlined in the previous section, has become elitist and arrogantly drunk with what they perceive to be unlimited power. Additionally, this erroneous belief – that there are no limits to their authority – lends itself to fiscal and ideological encroachment into the sovereign freedoms of both the individual states and the citizenry, freedoms previously guaranteed by what the professional elected class and its sycophant bureaucracy believes is an increasingly irrelevant US Constitution.

At our nation's outset, the one point where everyone was in agreement, the consensus among all who dared to pick up arms to forge the Great American Experiment, was this. Individualism was the unique element in our society that established us as sovereign people. It didn't matter the subject – religion, speech, thought, privacy, politics, each American citizen, each free and sovereign citizen to each of the coalescing 13 colonies was guaranteed, in the Bill of Rights, the freedom to be individually unique, and the liberty to exist devoid of unenumerated government interference.

Today, we exist as a country, as a citizenry, whose constitutionally guaranteed rights to religion, free speech, thought, privacy, and politics are aggressively under siege from our own government and its powerful allies in the public-private sector, chiefly in the BigTech and financial sectors.

Ideologues and opportunists, who have exploited the Machiavellian tactic of "divide and rule," continuously craft loosely-worded legislation that allows Executive Branch bureaucrats to flesh out the minutia via regulatory language,[28] extending the federal government's power and purview over the people, even as they assess new means by which to regulate, manipulate, and tax the people to advance and finance special interest ventures of opportunism.

With each new Congress come more poorly written pieces of legislation and overreaching restrictions that encroach on our freedom of thought and, through that, our freedom of speech. Our federal government – and their servile supporters – utilizes a shadow set of rules for us to live by, rules steeped in political correctness (read: wokeness), an ever-morphing set of definitions that guard a Marxist-based totalitarian agenda of transformation from a Constitutional Republic to an elitist and globalist oligarchy.

The ever-morphing Marxist elements of political correctness are – and always have been – antithetical to the liberties and freedoms guaranteed to every citizen of the United States via compact in the US Constitution and the Bill of Rights. Not until recently has the professional political class set itself to codify these contradictions to freedom into law.[29]

---

[28] https://lawliberty.org/why-congress-cedes-power-to-the-administrative-state/

[29] https://www.cato.org/commentary/hate-speech-laws-are-unconstitutional-harmful-democracy

Together with their public-private partnership allies in BigTech and the private sector, the professional governmental class is actively engaged in destroying the citizenry's guaranteed right to redress of government by refusing to confront the communications behemoths of Silicon Valley in their blatant and oppressive censorship of the American people.[30]

And, we are starting to see the underpinnings of the dark influence the government-aligned financial sector has on our freedoms – freedoms of religion, free speech, thought, privacy, and politics. In their deplatforming and "depersonalization" of individuals through the refusal of service – including access to financial means, solely based on ideology and politics, they are engaged in controlling our right to free speech, freedom of movement, and redress of government.[31]

When the government can partner with entities that control your speech and finances to coerce you into falling silent in your redress of government, or to bully you into altering your thinking, we have lost the freedoms guaranteed to us in the Bill of Rights; we have lost our guaranteed right to free thought, to individualism.

When the government and her allies *control our rights*, the government is lord and master, and the American people are *not* being served by our government.

[30] https://nypost.com/2022/10/23/lawsuit-reveals-vast-censorship-scheme-by-big-tech-and-the-federal-government/

[31] https://fee.org/resources/what-is-cancel-culture-getting-beyond-the-partisan-talking-points/

PROBLEM NO. 3 | A GOVERNMENT BEHOLDEN TO AN IDEOLOGICAL AGENDA

In the expansion of its power and the institution's fall to the disingenuously opportunistic, the government of the United States has ceased being about executing representative government on behalf of the citizens. It has, instead, become an ideologically driven tool of social engineering and elitist wealth generation for an oligarchic ruling class.

Regardless of political party – although it is demonstrative on the political Left, the majority of those elected to federal office are increasingly more concerned with special interest appeasement and their party's ideological agendas than in executing good government for the whole of the American people. They comprise what many are describing as the "Uniparty".[32]

For the most part, the days of elected representatives going to Washington, DC to represent the people of their districts or the states is over.

Where the political Left is dangerously courting the failed philosophy of Marxism, affecting its transformative stricture through the use of political correctness (wokeness), identity politics, and social and racial justice movements, the political Right is invested in the crony-capitalist establishment structure that many refer to as

---

[32] https://www.conservapedia.com/Uniparty

the Deep State; the bureaucratic status quo that "does lunch" on K Street.

Regardless of their juxtaposition politically and ideologically, both political parties at the federal level – the Uniparty – have tantamount to absolved themselves from their constitutionally mandated duty to serve the people; to execute, with fidelity, service to the people. Instead, they have placed themselves *above* the people, making politically expedient deals and passing legislation that continuously encroaches on the constitutional freedoms our nation's citizens were guaranteed as sacrosanct.

Additionally, both ideological factions are greedily seeking positions of leadership on the global government stage. With each inroad the Left and Right make in the quest for this leadership among the Davos crowd,[33] they become increasingly willing and agreeable to the surrender of our freedoms and national sovereignty and, along with it, the sovereign rights of the citizenry.

An excellent example of how our federally elected officials have turned their backs on the American people is in their embrace of the World Economic Forum's Great Reset.[34] This dangerous vehicle is crafted to place an oligarchic privileged class over all the sovereign nations of the world via public-private partnerships where the global elite use their leverage in the private sector – and

[33] https://www.weforum.org/

[34] https://imprimis.hillsdale.edu/what-is-the-great-reset/

especially in banking with the digitization of currencies – with the full cooperation of the nations' governments, to reshape the world to one of their vision.

Make no mistake, the Great Reset is a vehicle that will destroy our constitutionally protected freedoms. Today, our federal government is copacetic with the Great Reset.

Our elected political class is so invested in winning the political games – both in Washington, DC, and on the global stage, that they are constantly and continuously failing the American people.

In its transformative quest for power and global influence, the Left is threatening the very tenants of the Bill of Rights and, specifically, the right to free speech, the right to redress government, the right to bear arms, the right to religious freedom, and the right to be free from unreasonable search, among others.

The Right, in its defense of what has become the federal bureaucratic status quo in the United States, ignores any organic attempt at restoring the sovereignty of the states as mandated by the US Constitution. Less overtly than the Left, the Right chips away at our freedoms by enacting legislation that continuously adds pages to an already bloated federal registry.

And both parties; both factions, jealously guard their monopoly of power in tandem. As exemplified in the 2020 election cycle, nothing is off the table when a political outsider threatens the status quo.

To that end, the uniquely American ideal of anyone being able to become President of the United States is, for the most part, a lie. In order to become President, one must embrace the ideologies of the political classes and, even then, unless the person is an anointed member of one of the parties, there is little chance of an outsider's election to the presidency.

Again, President Washington warned the country in his Farewell Address about the dangers of political factions in government, saying they would be the demise of the Republic. Today, we have a system of politics that rules the country, not government of, by, and for the people.

Today, the American people are *not* being served by our government.

55

WE HAVE LOST FREEDOMS & REPRESENTATIVE GOVERNMENT

"If it is true that the basic quest of man is freedom, the question we must ask is: Is it freedom from or freedom for?"

– Marcus Tullius Cicero

The consequences deriving from the many problems facing our nation – as well as the divisive issues created by the Machiavellian opportunists, are that we have ceased existing as a true Constitutional Republic. We have long ago ceased existing as the government the Framers bequeathed us, that structure died with the Wilson administration. And if we continue on the current path we will, without fail, witness the fundamental transformation of the United States of America from a Constitutional Republic to Democratic Socialism and then to a Socialist and then Communist nation in total.

We ceased being a Constitutional Republic as bequeathed by our Forefathers when Progressives (today more accurately recognized as Marxists but actually existing as neo-fascists) pushed through the ratification of the 17th Amendment. That amendment provided for the citizenry's direct election of US Senators.

With the ratification of the 17th Amendment, the United States Senate became a politicized body rather than a body whose sole purpose and interest was protecting the sovereignty of the individual states and the constitutions of those states. The US Senate was – at its inception – meant to be the firewall that thwarted and obstructed an out-of-control and overreaching federal government. With the ratification of the 17th Amendment – and the complete politicization of that chamber, the Senate has enjoined in that corruptive overreach.

With the ratification of the 17th Amendment, in tandem with several controversial and activist Supreme Court rulings that expanded the authority of the federal government over the states via the Commerce and Supremacy Clauses, the federal government has been able to completely contort and/or destroy the necessary balance of federalism and anti-federalism that resulted in our Constitutional Republic.

State constitutions have been routinely marginalized, diminished, and outright ignored, as has the sovereignty of the states and their peoples. Ideological and politically-based mandates crafted and enacted in one state, lobbied by well-funded activist groups at the federal level, routinely become unfunded federal mandates onto the rest of the states and, therefore, the country as a whole, where the wealth of people in one state or region is captured by an authoritative centralized government to fund said mandates in other states without the indigenous resources to execute the mandates.

Predominantly Left-leaning urban centers in several states – namely, but not limited to California, New York, and Illinois – routinely bleed the federal treasury because of their own financial malfeasance and irresponsibility; malfeasance that is the result of irresponsible and poorly thought-out spendthrift ideological initiatives whose legitimacy is *not* found in the US Constitution under the notion of "common good," and by blatant political opportunism.

And with an ignorant but no less potent movement to marginalize and eventually end the Electoral College in the election of President and Vice President of the United

States, the protection of the minority's right to individualism; to Americanism – as guaranteed by the very idea *of* a Constitutional Republic and representative government, is ended.[35]

This unconstitutional and massive transformative overreach by both political parties – at every level, and all branches, departments, agencies, bureaus, and commissions of the federal government – has delivered us to this point in time when politics has replaced government, and ideological privilege steeped in elitism usurps the right of every individual to equal opportunity, right, and access to the preservation of "life, liberty, and the pursuit of happiness".

The consequences of the problems and manipulation that face our Republic have, without doubt, been achieved. We the People, the sovereign citizens of the United States who were bequeathed a right to individualism, have become servants to a spendthrift government that no longer represents its people but instead represents its own best interests. The American people are not being served by our government.

[35] https://www.brookings.edu/policy2020/bigideas/its-time-to-abolish-the-electoral-college/

SUCCUMBING TO A GOVERNMENT OF CENTRAL PLANNING

"The right to 'liberty' and 'pursuit' of happiness is incompatible with a government that makes choices for you."

– A.E. Samaan

Bureaucracy is the inevitable byproduct of an all-powerful centralized government; a government with an addiction to gathering power. In the United States, the federal bureaucracy (sometimes referred to as the "Deep State" or "The Swamp") refers to the convoluted system of Executive Branch administrative organizations, procedures, and connected entities that create, implement, and enforce policies through regulation; policies with the weight of laws created without going through a comprehensive and constitutionally mandated legislative process.

By understanding the historical context; the genesis of our current federal bureaucratic quagmire – even in a cursory form, we can begin to understand the complexities and challenges inherent in bureaucratic governance and explore potential avenues for reform.

The American colonial experience under empirical British rule would leave a lasting stain on our developing nation in the form of the employment of bureaucracy in our halls of government. The British administrative system – a system more fitting to a monarchy – provided a legacy foundation for American governance structures, with influences evident in the creation of myriad Executive Branch departments, agencies, and entities and the adoption of bureaucratic practices.

With the ratification of the US Constitution and the seating of our federal government in 1789, the Executive Branch began to create departments to handle specific policy areas. The Departments of State, Treasury, and

War, among others, formed the early nucleus of the bureaucratic apparatus. The growth of these departments laid the groundwork for future expansion into the quagmire of bureaucratic red tape we now suffer under today and exemplifies the difficult relationship the citizenry and the states have with the federal government.

In the early years of the Republic, the spoils system,[36] a practice of political patronage, became prevalent and widespread; seemingly ever-expanding. This system allowed elected officials to appoint supporters to bureaucratic positions, often based on loyalty rather than merit. The spoils system not only posed challenges to the efficiency and professionalism of those who were selectively tasked with "serving the people," it created the federal bureaucracy that today has fealty to the elected class; the elitist class, rather than a devout loyalty to the people.

The late 19th and early 20th centuries witnessed rapid industrialization and urbanization, allowing for a moment in time when federal government intervention was perceived to be a necessity to address social and economic issues. This era, known as the Progressive Era, brought about so-called reforms couched as the federal government taking aim at curbing corruption, improving public services, and creating level playing fields for the people. In fact, this era served to introduce an unprecedented expansion of the scope of the federal

---

[36] https://www.encyclopedia.com/history/united-states-and-canada/us-history/spoils-system

government's authority and the widespread expansion of bureaucratic institutions.

Aggressively pursuing a transformative agenda, Progressive "reformers," including President Woodrow Wilson, sought to increase and expand academically fueled bureaucracy[37] in the federal government under the pretext of "deferring to the experts." Under this deference to the country's academic elite, Wilson's administration facilitated the creation of what would become today's civil service protections for appointees and employees of the federal government; an "unfireable" protected class that ushered in the politicization of government at a national level.[38]

The Progressive Era also facilitated the creation of a cadre of regulatory agencies, such as the Interstate Commerce Commission and the Food & Drug Administration.[39] These agencies were tasked with overseeing specific industries and ensuring fair practices; fair as the *bureaucracy* would define. The creation of these regulatory agencies marked a significant shift in the role of the bureaucracy, transitioning from primarily administrative functions to regulatory oversight; regulatory oversight that would increasingly replace the required legislative processes mandated by the Constitution to create the power of law.

[37] https://www.heritage.org/the-constitution/commentary/unaccountable-bureaucrats-experts-interfere-popular-sovereignty

[38] https://jebkinnison.com/2016/04/13/civil-service-woodrow-wilsons-progressive-dream/

[39] https://www.heritage.org/political-process/report/the-birth-the-administrative-state-where-it-came-and-what-it-means-limited

Under Wilson's reign, the nation also finally succumbed to the creation of a "public-private partnership" that would literally change the world.

In 1913, the first successful central bank of the United States was created in the Federal Reserve System. This financial entity consisted of a tightly controlled group of the nation's (and the world's) wealthiest banks that colluded with the federal government to administer the nation's banking system and, thus, control its wealth. To fully understand the collusive nature of this relationship and the detrimental impact of its existence on the worth of money, read *The Creature from Jekyll Island* by G. Edward Griffin.[40]

The Great Depression of the 1930s opened the door for a massive expansion of government intervention into the domain of the free market and the private sector. President Franklin D. Roosevelt's New Deal signified a significant turning point in American governance, with the federal government assuming – assuming being the operative word here – a more dominating and authoritative role in economic and social affairs.[41]

The New Deal era achieved the creation of collectivist social welfare programs such as Social Security (which in its original form was supposed to eventually convert to privately managed annuities managed by each citizen)

[40] https://amzn.to/3lVr7bM

[41] https://www.fff.org/2009/01/14/socialism-fascism-deal/

and the establishment of the Works Progress Administration. The explained purpose of these programs was to provide security, relief, recovery, and reform and required the expansion of bureaucratic institutions for "administrative purposes".

The New Deal also saw the creation of a plethora of federal administrative agencies, such as the Securities & Exchange Commission and the Federal Deposit Insurance Corporation, both closely associated with the Federal Reserve Banking System. These agencies were designed to regulate financial markets and restore confidence in the banking system.

The expansion of the authority of the federal government's Executive Branch in the creation of institutionalized bureaucracy during this period reflected the federal government's avarice for power, couching their greed for power as the elected class addressing the changing needs of society and crisis response.

The pre-Cold War era through the subsequent postwar period facilitated a significant expansion of the federal bureaucracy. This expansion was driven largely by national security concerns and made common the phrase coined by outgoing President, Dwight D. Eisenhower, "the military-industrial complex".[42] Agencies such as the Central Intelligence Agency and the National Aeronautics & Space Administration emerged during this time,

[42] https://www.archives.gov/milestone-documents/president-dwight-d-eisenhowers-farewell-address#transcript

reflecting the federal government's increased focus on defense, intelligence, and scientific research.

The federal workforce (read: the bureaucracy or the "Deep State" or "The Swamp") expanded substantially in the postwar period, with increased demands for administrative and technical expertise. The growth of the bureaucracy, the elected and administrative class argued, allowed government to respond to new challenges and emerging policy areas, such as environmental protection with the creation of the Environmental Protection Agency, and civil rights with the expansion of the Department of Justice into the area of determining right and wrong in matters of race, racism, and gender discrimination.

Technological advancements, particularly in information and communication technologies born out of the space race and the military-industrial complex, further contributed to the growth of bureaucratic institutions. But while the computerization of administrative processes and the advent of digital record-keeping systems enhanced efficiency and, therefore opened the door for the *downsizing* of the federal government bureaucracy, the elected and administrative class instead *expanded* the scope of bureaucratic functions.

The federal bureaucracy's expanding role in federal governance has rightfully faced criticism for its inefficiencies, red tape, cost, and lack of accountability. Critics successfully argue that excessive regulations and administrative procedures hinder innovation, responsiveness, and effective policy implementation, disenfranchising much of the citizenry from entering the marketplace, thus denying them the fruits of the free market and the acquisition of the American Dream.

The advent of Silicon Valley information technology has had a profound impact on bureaucratic governance, both good and bad. E-government initiatives, digitization of administrative processes, and the use of data analytics have introduced the potential to enhance efficiency, transparency, and citizen self-service and engagement. However, technological advancements have failed to reduce the size of the bureaucracy even as it brings new challenges, such as data security and privacy concerns.

Additionally, the federal government's bureaucratic agencies allow for unchecked administrative discretion in interpreting and implementing policies. This wide-latitude discretion allows for the coercive and opportunistic shaping of outcomes of policies and their impact on society. It raises concerns about – and has exemplified – the potential for unelected officials to exert significant influence over policy decisions and, therefore, regulatory impacts that hold the unlegislated weight of law. One need only consider the existence and workings of "administrative courts" to understand the slippery slope that uncontrolled bureaucracy facilitates.[43]

The bureaucracy of our federal government exists within the framework of a system of government created to be

---

[43] https://cei.org/blog/what-are-administrative-law-courts-why-do-they-matter/

representative; where accountability to elected representatives and the public is not only essential but is also constitutionally mandated. To date, the slippery slope of striking a balance between bureaucratic expertise and constitutionally-mandated oversight has resulted in the bureaucracy's growing authority and the growing authority of the Executive Branch on each and every American citizen; an authority that has been *assumed* and not legislated.

73

NULLIFICATION

A COUNTRY RULED BY 'EXPERTS'

"Nothing would be more fatal than for the Government of States to get in the hands of experts. Expert knowledge is limited knowledge, and the unlimited ignorance of the plain man who knows where it hurts is a safer guide than any rigorous direction of a specialized character."

– Winston Churchill

Academics argue that bureaucracy is a necessary component of modern government; of government that is relatable to the "new normal" global order. They insist that a measured bureaucracy facilitates the responsible implementation of policies, the provision of public services, and the assurance of administrative efficiency. However, the extent to which bureaucracy and rule by bureaucracy can both hinder the effectiveness of representative government and also replace it is a matter of concern.

Representative government – as our Constitutional Republic was created to provide – aims to reflect the will of the people, allowing citizens to both participate in the decision-making processes through elected representatives and to serve as the "rudder" for the direction of our country. But bureaucracy, when unchecked – overly burdensome, and/or co-opted by the corrupt, can undermine the principles of representative government and cede control of the nation to an unelected privileged class of elites who exist beholden to special interests rather than to the service of the people.

To comprehend the negative impact of bureaucracy on representative government, it is important to understand its nature and characteristics. Bureaucracy is characterized by a hierarchical structure, division of labor, formal rules, and adherence to standard operating procedures. While these aspects are necessary for organizational efficiency, those involved in executing the duties charged by the organizations, agencies, and departments that comprise that bureaucracy must do so with fidelity to the fact that they owe their existence to the people. When any part of that metric fails, bureaucracy can impede the functioning of representative government.

The bureaucratic structure of the US federal government most often operates independently of the popular will. This is because those who constitute the bureaucracy – the civil service class of the federal government – see themselves as answerable to the elected class rather than to the people; to the Executive Branch of the federal government rather than to the citizenry. So, the distance and the authoritative pathway between the bureaucracy and the citizens are significant. This can lead to a lack of accountability and responsiveness as well as a sense of superiority toward the people; unelected bureaucrats, driven by their own interests and institutional inertia, resist or dilute the policies and preferences of elected representatives, thereby weakening the process of representative government and constitutionalism.

The federal government's bureaucratic apparatus is notorious for its complex regulations, convoluted procedures, and excessive red tape. Such administrative burdens can slow down decision-making processes, obstruct the implementation of policies, and discourage and even disenfranchise citizen engagement. Excessive bureaucratic requirements – under which we currently exist in almost every facet of our lives – can deter ordinary citizens from participating in governance, limiting the representative nature *of* the government.

The adherence to formal rules and standard procedures by bureaucratic entities often results in slow decision-making processes and/or the misapplication of regulatory constraints. These delays and constraints can have adverse consequences in times of crisis and immediacy when prompt action is required, resulting in an unresponsive government failing to serve the people.

The rigid structure of bureaucracy can also stifle innovation and adaptability because bureaucrats are often bound by established protocols and rules, making it difficult to respond creatively to emerging challenges and changing political, societal, and ideological landscapes. Representative government *must* be dynamic, capable of evolving and responding to societal changes in a reasonable and responsible measure of time. The inflexible nature of bureaucracy, therefore, can inhibit the necessary agility for effective governance. This is another point in a long line that validates the notion that the most effective and efficient level of government is the level *closest* to the people being governed.

Additionally, accountability mechanisms for bureaucratic structures can be complicated by the diffusion of responsibility among numerous and sometimes malaligned actors. When decision-making processes involve multiple layers of bureaucracy, it becomes challenging to pinpoint the individuals charged with oversight of the responsibility for outcomes, making it easier for officials to evade accountability. This diffusion of responsibility; this abdication of responsibility undermines the democratic principle of holding elected representatives answerable to the people.

Further, the federal government bureaucracy, due to its employment of the Wilsonian notion of "expertise" – and because of its protected longevity, are susceptible to capture by special interest groups. These groups often seek to influence bureaucratic decision-making to serve their own opportunistic and financially beneficial agendas. When bureaucracy becomes captured, it can undermine the impartiality and fairness of government actions, compromising the democratic principles of equal representation and justice.

A perfect example of the dangers in empowering an "expert class" to usurp the constitutional representation mandated by the US Constitution comes to us in the way the federal government – and several more liberal state governments – responded to the COVID pandemic. The federal government's response ceded all critical decision-making to the expert class, an expert class that, over the years, became deeply commingled with not only the private sector BigPharma institutions, but intertwined with what President Eisenhower described as the military industrial complex.

In May of 2023, Dr. David Martin[44], a Fellow of the Batten Institute at the Darden Graduate School of Business Administration at the University of Virginia, along with a host of other authoritative and critical voices on the

---

[44] https://www.davidmartin.world/about/

subject of the global COVID pandemic response to include Dr. Robert Malone[45] – the inventor of mRNA vaccine technology for which he holds a patent, spoke at the International COVID Summit, Part III[46] presented to the European Union Parliament. There, he spoke on the subject of the complexity of the convoluted and collusive relationships between the expert class that completely mishandled the COVID response, the federal government, and BigPharma.

The text below are excerpts from his talk at the summit:

> *"The [COVID] pandemic that we alleged to have happened in the last few years...did not happen overnight. In fact, the very specific pandemic using coronavirus began at a very different time.*

> *"Most of you don't know that coronavirus, as a model of a pathogen, was isolated in 1965. Coronavirus was identified in 1965 as one of the first infectious replicable viral models that could be used to modify a series of other experiences; the Human Condition. It was isolated, once upon a time, and associated with the common cold. But what's particularly interesting about its isolation in 1965 was that it was immediately identified as a pathogen that could be used and modified for a whole host of reasons, and you heard me correctly. That was 1965...*

---

[45] https://www.rwmalonemd.com/rna-vaccine-inventor

[46] https://www.internationalcovidsummit.com/

"In 1966, the very first coronavirus model was used as a transatlantic biological experiment in human manipulation. You heard the date, 1966. I hope you're getting the point of what I'm saying. This is not an overnight thing. This is actually something that's been long in the making. A year before I was born, we had the first transatlantic coronavirus data-sharing experiment between the United States and the United Kingdom and in 1967, the year I was born, we did the first human trials on inoculating people with modified Coronavirus...

"Fifty-six years ago. The overnight success of a pathogen that's been fifty-six years in engineering...in 1975, 1976, and 1977 we started figuring out how to modify coronavirus by putting it into different animals – pigs and dogs – and not surprisingly, by the time we got to 1990, we found out that coronavirus as an infectious agent was an industrial problem for two primary industries: the industries of dogs and pigs.

"Dog breeders and pig breeders found that coronavirus created gastrointestinal problems and that became the basis for Pfizer's first spike protein vaccine, patent filed – are you ready for this – in 1990...Pfizer. 1990. The very first spike protein vaccine for coronavirus...Isn't it fascinating that we were told that the spike protein is a 'new

thing,' 'we just found out'? That's the problem. We didn't 'just find out'.

"It was not just now...We found that out in 1990 and filed the first patents on vaccines in 1990 for the spike protein of coronavirus. And who would have thought Pfizer – clearly the innocent organization that does nothing but promote human health; clearly Pfizer – the organization that has not bought the votes in this chamber and every chamber of every government around the world, not that Pfizer, certainly they wouldn't have had anything to do with this!

"But oh yes, they did and in 1990 they found out that there was a problem with vaccines. They didn't work. Do you know why they didn't work? It turns out the coronavirus is a very malleable model. It transforms and it changes and it mutates over time. As a matter of fact, every publication on vaccines for coronavirus from 1990 until 2018 – every single publication – concluded that coronavirus escapes the vaccine impulse because it modifies and mutates too quickly for vaccines to be effective. And from 1990 to 2018, following the science is their own indictment of their own programs that said it doesn't work and there are thousands of publications to that effect – not a few hundred and not paid for by pharmaceutical companies. These are publications that are independent scientific research that shows unequivocally – including

efforts of the chimera modifications made by Ralph Baric at the University of North Carolina-Chapel Hill – all of them show vaccines do not work on coronavirus. That's the science and that science has never been disputed.

"But then we had an interesting development. In 2002 – and this date is most important because in 2002, the University of North Carolina-Chapel Hill patented – and I quote 'an infectious replication defective clone of coronavirus'.

"Listen to those words: 'infectious replication defective'. What does that phrase actually mean? For those of you not familiar with the language let me unpack it for you. Infectious replication defective means a weapon. It means something meant to target an individual but not have collateral damage to other individuals. That's what infectious replication defective means. And that patent was filed in 2002 on work funded by NIAID's Anthony Fauci from 1999 to 2002. That work, patented at the University of North Carolina-Chapel Hill, mysteriously preceded SARS 1.0 by a year.

"'Dave, are you suggesting that SARS 1.0 wasn't from a wet market in Wuhan? Are you suggesting it might have come from a laboratory at the University of North Carolina-Chapel Hill?'

"No, I'm not suggesting it. I'm telling you that's the fact.

"We engineered SARS. SARS is not a naturally occurring phenomenon. A naturally occurring phenomenon is called the common cold; it's called influenza-like illness; it's called gastroenteritis. That's the naturally occurring coronavirus. SARS is the research developed by humans weaponizing a life system model to actually attack human beings and they patented it in 2002.

"And in 2003, giant surprise, the CDC filed the patent on coronavirus isolated from humans in violation, once again, of biological and chemical weapons treaties and laws that we have in the United States...

"[L]et's get something very clear. When the CDC, in April of 2003, filed the patent on the SARS coronavirus isolated from humans what did they do? They downloaded a sequence from China and filed a patent on it in the United States.

"Any of you familiar with biological and chemical weapons treaties knows that's a violation; that's a crime. That's not an innocent oops. That's a crime.

"The United States patent office went as far as to reject that patent application on two occasions

until the CDC decided to bribe the patent office to override the patent examiner to ultimately issue the patent in 2007 on SARS coronavirus.

"It turns out that coronavirus was actually identified as a bio-terrorism threat in the European Union-sponsored events in 2002 and 2003, 20 years ago. That happened here in Brussels and across Europe.

"In 2005, this particular pathogen was specifically labeled as a bio-terrorism and bio-weapon platform technology, described as such – that's not my terminology, it was actually described as a bio-weapons platform technology in 2005. And from 2005 onwards it was actually classified as a bio-warfare enabling agent, its official classification from 2005 forward. I don't know if that sounds like 'public health' to you, does it? Biological warfare enabling technology designed to take out humanity, that's what it feels like and it feels like that because that's exactly what it is.

"We have been lured into believing that EcoHealth Alliance and DARPA and all of these organizations are what we should be pointing to. But we've been specifically requested to ignore the facts that over 10 billion dollars have been funneled through Black Operations through the check of Anthony Fauci who has a balance sheet and next to it is a bio-defense balance sheet equivalent. And it's been going on since 2005...

"In the fall of 2014, the University of North Carolina-Chapel Hill received a letter from NAID saying that while the gain of function moratorium on coronavirus in vivo should be suspended because their grants had already been funded, they received an exemption. Did you hear what I just said? A biological weapons lab facility at the University of North Carolina-Chapel Hill received an exemption from the gain of function moratorium so that by 2016 we could publish the journal article that said SARS coronavirus is poised for 'human emergence' in 2016...Was the coronavirus poised for human emergence? It was.

"The Wuhan Institute of Urology virus 1.0 [was pronounced to be] poised for human emergence in 2016 at the proceedings of the National Academy of Sciences such that by the time we get to 2017 and 2018, the following phrase entered into common parlance among the community: 'There is going to be an accidental or intentional release of a respiratory pathogen'.

"The operative word obviously in that phrase, is the word 'release'. Does that sound like 'leak'? Does that sound like a bat and a penguin went into a bar in the Wuhan market and hung out and had sex and low-and-behold we got SARS COVID 2? No. 'Accidental or intentional release of a respiratory pathogen' was the terminology

used four times in April of 2019, seven months before the allegation of patient number one for patent applications in Maderna where modified to include the term 'accidental or intentional release of respiratory pathogen' as the justification for making a vaccine for a thing that did not exist.

"Please make sure that you make reference in every investigation to the premeditation nature of this because it was in September 2019 that the world was informed that we were going to have an 'accidental or intentional release of respiratory pathogen' so that by September 2020 there would be a worldwide acceptance of a universal vaccine template. That's their words...the intent was to get the world to accept a universal vaccine template and the intent was to use coronavirus to get there...

"Let's read the last slide...we have to read this into the record:

"'Everywhere I go, until an infectious disease crisis is very real, present, and at the emergency threshold, it is often largely ignored to sustain the funding base beyond the crisis...we need to increase the public understanding for the need for medical countermeasures such as a pan-influenza or pan coronavirus vaccine...A key driver is the media and the economics will follow. We need to use that hype to our advantage.

Investors will respond if they see profit at the end of the process.'

"This was premeditated domestic terrorism stated at the proceedings of the National Academy of Sciences in 2015. This is an act of biological and chemical warfare perpetrated on the Human Race and it was admitted to in writing that this was a financial heist and a financial fraud. 'Investors will follow if they see profit at the end of the process'.

"Nature was hijacked. This whole story started in 1965 when we decided to hijack a natural model and decide to start manipulating it. Science was hijacked.

"When the only questions that could be asked were questions authorized under the patent protection of the CDC, the FDA, the NIH, and their equivalent organizations around the world, we didn't have independent science. We had hijacked science and, unfortunately, it was no moral oversight. It was a violation of all of the codes that we stand for. There was no independent financially disinterested independent review board ever impaneled around coronavirus, not once, not once. Not since 1965.

"We do not have a single independent IRB ever impaneled around coronavirus. So, morality was suspended for medical countermeasures, and,

ultimately, humanity was lost because we decided to allow it to happen.

"Our job today is to say...no more corporate patronage of science for their own self-interest unless they assume 100 percent product liability for every injury and every death that they maintain."

Now that the truth about how the COVID pandemic was mitigated by the federal government – now that we know as fact that the whole of the event was a profit scheme hatched through a public-private collusive partnership between BigPharma and the bureaucracy of the federal government with the corporate media complex running interference, we can fully appreciate the vulnerabilities our Republic faces at allowing the "expert class" to run roughshod over the governmental process.

91

THE ULTIMATE CONSEQUENCE:
A REPUBLIC LOST TO FASCISM

"It's not an endlessly expanding list of rights – the 'right' to education ,the 'right' to health care, the 'right' to food and housing. That's not freedom, that's dependency. Those aren't rights, those are the rations of slavery; hay and a barn for human cattle."

– Alexis de Tocqueville

It can be well-argued that the United States of America ceased being the nation with the form of government our Framers created for us with the codification of both the 17th Amendment, allowing for the direct election of US Senators by the people, and the institution of a behemoth Executive Branch bureaucracy.

The removal of protections granted to the states by the ability for each state's legislatures to appoint senators to the United States Senate fully politicized the federal government, leaving the institution prey to any and all political opportunists.

And because our nation's Executive Branch employs a bureaucratic system of operation and the Legislative Branch cedes legislative powers to the bureaucracy's regulatory apparatus, it can be accurately stated that our federal government is vulnerable to transformation at the will of special interests, nefarious actors, and to even those of with an eye toward revolution.

The traditional definition of fascism, according to Merriam-Webster, reads:

> *"...a political philosophy, movement, or regime (such as that of the Fascisti) that exalts nation and often race above the individual and that stands for a centralized autocratic government headed by a dictatorial leader, severe economic*

and social regimentation, and forcible
suppression of opposition..." [47]

Additionally, fascism, as evidenced by its execution during Mussolini's reign in Italy, relied heavily on the use of the private sector to fulfill agenda items that Mussolini's government couldn't legitimately impose onto the Italian people. To express this in 21st Century vernacular, the fascism of Mussolini employed public-private partnerships to execute an end-around to the Italian governmental process. What he couldn't achieve through the legitimate execution of government, he achieved through the coercion of the people through the force of the private sector.

One should see the frightening parallels to Mussolini's fascism in the US federal government's use of public-private partnerships and the Executive Branch's abuse of executive orders today. It would be a legitimate statement to describe our form of government today as neo-fascism shrouded in the mask of representative government.

The transformation of a Constitutional Republic to a fascist form of governance – or a neo-fascist government as is the case today in the United States – is a complex process that sees a gradual erosion of democratic institutions and the rise of authoritarian ideologies. This rise requires certain socio-political conditions to exist, the

[47] https://www.merriam-webster.com/dictionary/fascism

use of psyops/propaganda[48], a charismatic message of leadership, and the consolidation of power, this is and always has been achievable in any nation through the history of man and, thus a vulnerability laying within any society.

A constitutional government, characterized by the rule of law, separation of powers, and protection of individual rights, is considered a hallmark of democracy. This is the government that was created for the American people in the advent of our Republic. However, history has witnessed instances where such systems gradually deteriorated into fascist regimes, marked by totalitarian and authoritarian control (less the will of the people), suppression of any kind of dissent, and the concentration of power in the hands of a single ruler, ruling party, ruling ideology, or oligarchy.

Constitutional governments encompass fundamental principles such as the rule of law, checks and balances, protection of individual rights, and democratic decision-making processes while promoting political pluralism, accountability, and the protection of civil liberties. Fascism is a highly authoritarian political ideology characterized by dictatorial power, strong pseudo-nationalism, suppression of any type of dissent, and the subordination of individual rights to the interests of the state (think: "You need to get vaccinated for the common good"). Fascist regimes often exhibit aggressive

---

[48] https://rwmalonemd.substack.com/p/behavioral-control

militarism, state-controlled economies, and the promotion of a single-party system.

It doesn't take much to see the poison fruit of the tree of fascism in many elements of today's United States:

- Woke ideology is championed by an aggressively expanding federal government counter to a lopsided public denunciation of that ideology even as the colluding private sector elites impose wokeism on the people.

- Any dissent against any preferred narrative – narratives anointed by the woke elite – are immediately censored, ridiculed, and otherwise suppressed (read: canceled) by both the government and its public-private partners.

- Our individual rights, guaranteed by the Bill of Rights, are now subject to interpretation leaving those rights definable by the authoritative ruling class.

- And lastly, we are seeing the militarization of federal law enforcement and intelligence agencies against the American people (recall parents at school board meetings being labeled "domestic terrorists")

All of these maladies exist today in our society and do so while the US Treasury and Federal Reserve scheme to create a Central Bank Digital Currency (CBDC), controllable by those in power.[49]

To comprehend the transformation from constitutional government to fascism (or in the case of today's United States, neo-fascism), we analyze three significant case studies: the Weimar Republic in Germany, Mussolini's Italy, and the Franco regime in Spain.

The Weimar Republic emerged in the aftermath of World War I in an attempt to establish a democratic system of government in Germany. However, economic instability, political polarization, and the one-sided Treaty of Versailles created an environment ripe for extremist ideologies to flourish among a devastated populace. Adolf Hitler and the Nazi Party exploited these vulnerabilities, employing psyops propaganda, cultural scapegoating, and charismatic leadership messaging to gradually nurture discontent among the people while they dismantled democratic institutions bit by bit to establish a fascist regime that, in the end, slaughtered tens of millions including Jews, Catholics, Gypsies, and homosexuals, among other demographics.

In post-World War I Italy, political discontent among the Italian people emanating from economic challenges and the perceived failure of liberal democracy provided fertile ground for Benito Mussolini's fledgling fascist movement. Mussolini capitalized on pseudo-nationalist sentiments and consolidated power through the March on Rome. He

[49] https://www.cato.org/study/risks-of-cbdcs

gradually achieved the transformation of Italy's government from one of representation into a one-party state, aggressively suppressing political opposition and establishing a totalitarian regime.

The Spanish Civil War (1936-1939) witnessed a clash between democratic forces and fascist factions led by Generalissimo Francisco Franco. After Franco's victory, Spain experienced the establishment of a repressive totalitarian regime characterized by censorship, political purges, and the suppression of regional identities.

Several common factors can contribute to the transformation from constitutional government to fascism.

Moderate to severe economic crises can create social unrest – especially in a society that promotes victimhood and nurtures entitlement, paving the way for radical or "revolutionary" ideologies to gain popularity. High unemployment, inflation, and perceived and propagandized inequality provide a breeding ground for disillusionment and resentment, making individuals more susceptible to extreme political movements. One need look no further in today's United States than the Black Lives Matter and LGBTQ+ Movements to see how nefarious players can prey on the desires of the intellectually vulnerable.[50]

Weak or fragmented political institutions make a constitutional government vulnerable to authoritarian

---

[50] https://www.washingtonexaminer.com/news/blms-millions-go-unaccounted-for-after-leaders-quietly-jump-ship

takeovers. Factions and infighting – such as we are seeing in both major political parties today – can paralyze decision-making processes, leaving a power vacuum in government and a frustrated populace that can be exploited by charismatic leaders seeking to sow discontent and consolidate support leading to authoritarian rule; to fascist rule; to neo-fascist rule, and in many cases to communism.

Constitutional governments may also suffer from systemic flaws, such as corruption, inadequate checks and balances, or inefficiencies in ensuring equal representation. Today these maladies are exemplified in an overtly corrupt federal government (and especially in the corrupted Executive and Legislative Branches), political factions that routinely attempt to delegitimize all aspects of government that do not advance their radical ideologies – such as the demonization of the US Supreme Court by elements of the radical Left over rulings adversely effecting the Left's special interests, and half of our country feeling as though the government has been hijacked away from our founding principles; taken by a new neo-fascism at the hands of the woke. These weaknesses erode public trust in democratic institutions, making it easier for fascist ideologies to gain traction.

Pysops and propaganda campaigns play a critical role in transforming public perception and manipulating popular opinion. Fascist and neo-fascist regimes employ sophisticated propaganda machinery to promote specific narratives, scapegoat groups that are not aligned with their agenda, and stifle dissenting voices, ultimately facilitating the erosion of democratic values. At no other time in American history has a more concerted effort to control how Americans think and say been executed than is being executed today.

One simply needs to recall the two years of manipulation the people suffered during the federal government's COVID response to the "heel order" of BigPharma to understand how vulnerable we are to a well-orchestrated psyops propaganda campaign.[51]

Other examples include the false narrative of systemic racism in law enforcement and the science-denying propaganda of Diversity, Inclusion, and Equity being executed on behalf of the LGBTQ+ movement as well as the demonization of the blockchain-based cryptocurrency sphere as "non-transparent" by the banking sector and the US Treasury Department.[52] [53]

The transition from constitutional government to fascism (or in terms related to today, neo-fascism) involves various mechanisms that consolidate power and suppress opposition:

A. Charismatic Leadership and Cult of Personality – Charismatic leaders who can exploit societal grievances and offer a vision of national

---

[51] https://rwmalonemd.substack.com/p/psywars

[52] https://www.heritage.org/gender/commentary/transgender-ideology-riddled-contradictions-here-are-the-big-ones

[53] https://tinyurl.com/4nkr7m7w

rejuvenation often serve as catalysts for the transformation to fascism. They cultivate a cult of personality, exuding confidence, and promising stability, which can lead to the erosion of the public's fidelity to democratic principles and the consolidation of power to the hands of the oppressor.

B. Suspension of Civil Liberties and Legal Protections – Those seeking to establish neo-fascist regimes systematically seek to undermine civil liberties, curtail freedom of speech, assembly, and association, and weaken independent institutions. They seek to subvert or suspend legal protections to facilitate a totalitarian government with broad powers to suppress dissent and control public discourse.

C. Centralization of Power and Suppression of Opposition – Those seeking to establish neo-fascist regimes seek to consolidate power by centralizing authority within the ruling party or leader. They quest to dismantle democratic institutions, suppress political opposition, and establish mechanisms of control such as secret police forces or paramilitary organizations.

Examining historical case studies and the factors and mechanisms involved in the transformation from a constitutional form of government to fascism provides valuable lessons and warning signs for those sensible and *honest* enough to see them. These oversight obligations include monitoring economic stability, fostering and supporting strong democratic institutions, promoting media literacy, and actively safeguarding civil liberties.

Sadly, today, it can be argued that a majority of Americans are more concerned with the many aspects of their daily personal lives than in allocating time to the one responsibility they have as American citizens: governmental oversight.

So, while the transformation from a constitutional government to fascism – or neo-fascism – is a complex, multifaceted process, our nation – in its current state, societally – is failing to identify the key warning signs. We are failing to safeguard our democratic institutions. And we are – through our apathy to oversight and engagement – failing to prevent the erosion of our fundamental rights and freedoms. We are *not* vigilant. We do *not* actively promote democratic values. And we are *definitely not* counteracting the forces that seek to undermine the very foundations of our Constitutional Republic.

SOLUTION-BASED THINKING: AN OVERVIEW OF A THREE-PRONGED SOLUTION

"The State governments possess inherent advantages, which will ever give them an influence and ascendancy over the national government, and will for ever preclude the possibility of federal encroachments. That their liberties, indeed, can be subverted by the federal head, is repugnant to every rule of political calculation."

– Alexander Hamilton

There are at least two fundamental actions that can be taken at the state level and three actions that can be enacted by a Convention of the States or through the State initiated amendment process to the US Constitution, that will avert a further fracturing of our nation. Should these actions be taken we may very well see a move back to constitutionality and a form of government closer to that which our Framers intended for the American people.

These five actions include the embrace of nullification, the re-routing of federal tax remittance, a move toward restructuring the constitutionally codified operations of the federal government without encroaching on the powers the US Constitution outlines for that governmental level, instituting stand-alone legislation practices, and mandated term-limits for all federally elected officials.

Chief among the needs required for any of this to be tenable is a will of state governors and legislators to dedicate themselves to the acquisition of these goals. Short of the full embrace of at least two of these critical measures – nullification and a re-routing of federal tax remittance – this conjoined solution has no possibility of succeeding.

NULLIFICATION |
EMPLOYING THE SANCTUARY STATE MODEL
The argument over whether nullification is a constitutional possibility has been an ongoing one since the first state

challenge to federal law. But the fact remains that nullification is at the very heart of the 10th Amendment in its stipulation that:

> *"The powers not delegated to the United States by the Constitution, nor prohibited by it to the States, are reserved to the States respectively, or to the people."*

By the very existence of this Amendment – in addition to the wording of the 9th Amendment, which specifically protects the rights of the individual, nullification by the states of unconstitutional federal law is not only legitimized but it is also codified.

Additionally, the federal government has already established the precedent of tolerating the nullification of federal law by the states in the existence of sanctuary states; sanctuary status that applies to a variety of issues.

With regard to immigration, according to the Federation for American Immigration Reform, eleven states and over 600 jurisdictions already consider themselves sanctuary states where the issue of federal immigration law is concerned.[54] These states are:

- California
- Colorado
- Connecticut

[54] https://www.fairus.org/issue/sanctuary-policies/do-you-live-1-11-sanctuary-states

- Illinois
- Massachusetts
- New Jersey
- New Mexico
- New York
- Oregon
- Vermont
- Washington

By definition – and using the argument of immigration as an example, a sanctuary state is a state which actively offers political support to undocumented immigrants through an official government capacity. This "official government capacity" includes, but is not limited to, any official governmental actions such as the passage of legislation or executive order.

Political statements, however, are not considered actions.

A perfect example of how nullification is used in the matter of immigration is exemplified in California, an immigration sanctuary state. That state's legislature nullified federal law in the form of California Senate Bill 54 of 2017 – otherwise known as the California Sanctuary State Bill,[55] which codified California as a sanctuary state, legalizing and standardizing statewide non-cooperation policies between California law enforcement agencies and federal immigration authorities.

[55] https://www.fairus.org/legislation/state-and-local-legislation/california-sanctuary-state-bill-sb-54-summary-and-history

Included in California's nullification of federal immigration law were these specific actions:

- Prohibits state and local law enforcement from holding illegal aliens on the basis of federal immigration detainers, or transferring them into federal custody, unless they've been convicted in the last 15 years for one of a list of 31 crimes, or are a registered sex offender: if not, they may only be held with a warrant from a federal judge

- Prohibits state and local law enforcement from asking anyone about their immigration status

- Prohibits state and local law enforcement from sharing any information with federal immigration authorities that is not available to the general public

- Prohibits state and local law enforcement from using any of their money or personnel to "investigate, interrogate, detain, detect, or arrest persons for immigration enforcement purposes"

- Prohibits state and local law enforcement from allowing federal immigration authorities to use space in their facilities

- Limits how and when state and local law enforcement can contract with federal immigration authorities

- Grants discretion to state and local law enforcement to cooperate even less with federal immigration authorities than the bill authorizes them to, but not more

This California law Is near-universally recognized and described by both its supporters and opponents as a sanctuary state bill. It protects those who have broken the law by illegally existing in the United States at the expense of citizens, increases illegal immigration to California, and sends the message that those who have broken the law to exist in the United States are welcome and will be protected everywhere in the state of California and at expense of the citizenry.

In the culmination of each of the provisions in California's Sanctuary State Bill working in tandem, federal immigration law is tantamount to unenforceable and, therefore, nullified.

This is a boilerplate for almost every other state sanctuary legislation and, by its very existence, represents a state's acknowledgment of its nullification powers.

Further, because the federal government has tolerated sanctuary state status in each of these 11 states since 2017, they have established a precedent of recognizing a state's right to claim sanctuary status, thus acknowledging each of these states' rights to nullification.

So, with the federal government tolerating sanctuary state status and the states enacting nullification of federal immigration law, the table is set for *any* state to effectively nullify *any* federal law that their state legislatures have evidenced to be at the very least unconstitutional, and at its greatest potency undesirable.

ELIMINATING PUNISHMENT |
RE-ROUTING REMITTANCE OF FEDERAL TAXES

I have stated this clearly to those with whom I have engaged on the issue. Minds much more versed in the law and the crafting of legislation than mine will be required to do some of the best work of their lives and, perhaps, the centerpiece of their lives work.

The only tool that the federal government has to prevent the states from invoking nullification is the denial of revenue. As it stands today, if a state were to invoke nullification the federal government in the form of the Executive Branch could immediately withhold funding for many federally-funded and partially-funded federal programs. This loss of revenue would serve as a federal "whip" to force the offending state back into capitulation making the federal government little more than an *ipso facto* overlord; slave master.

But what if the ability to withhold funding from a state were removed? What if there *wasn't* a need for a state to require federal funding for *any* cost or program afforded its citizens? What if smartly crafted state legislation turned the tables and withheld tax revenue directly emanating from its citizenry *to* the federal government, thus starving the federal government of its ability to both punish a state and also force it to subsidize its special interest-serving and spendthrift policies?

It is a fact, the income tax we all understand today wasn't codified until 1913 with the Progressive era Woodrow Wilson administration. The 16th Amendment, passed during Wilson's administration, reads:

> *"The Congress shall have power to lay and collect taxes on incomes, from whatever source derived, without apportionment among the several States, and without regard to any census or enumeration."* [56]

But while the income tax on individuals is often acknowledged as beginning with the passage of the 16th Amendment – passed by Congress on July 2, 1909, and ratified on February 3, 1913, there are instances where lawmakers attempted to saddle the American public with federal taxation years before.

Congress passed the Revenue Act of 1861[57] to help pay for the costs of the US Civil War only to see that codified law *repealed* just ten years later, something unheard of in present-day politics and government.

[56] https://www.archives.gov/founding-docs/amendments-11-27#xvi

[57] https://constitutioncenter.org/blog/say-happy-birthday-to-the-first-income-tax

Congress, never at a loss for wanting to spend other people's money, again attempted to levy a tax on individuals in 1894,[58] when they enacted a flat rate federal income tax. This was ruled unconstitutional the following year by the United States Supreme Court because it was a direct tax not apportioned according to the population of each state.

But in 1913, with the ratification of the 16th amendment, the objection of a non-apportioned tax was removed, allowing the federal government to tax the income of individuals without regard to the population of each state.

So, as you can see, there is a precedent for revoking the federal government's ability to levy taxes on the American people. It has already been done via a legitimate act of Congress and through the power of constitutional law.

As our current tax law is structured, every wage-earning American – whether through private or public means – is required to file a federal tax return with the Internal Revenue Service (IRS). These filings fulfill the reporting of income for each individual to the federal government and are used to calculate the taxes owed – if any – by the person(s) filing the returns.

The supposition being made here is that through the power of the legislative and/or amendment process at the state level, a measure could be crafted that

[58] https://www.encyclopedia.com/history/encyclopedias-almanacs-transcripts-and-maps/1894-income-tax-and-wilson-gorman-tariff-act

acknowledges the filing of an individual's tax return but prohibits that state's citizenry from *directly remitting* owed federal taxes *to* the federal government.

Instead, the state would task its state Treasury Department to algorithmically calculate the taxes due to the federal government, in proportion to its population, and summarily submit the taxes due from its citizens in bulk, doing so based on the *original* apportionment clause in the US Constitution:

> *"...direct taxes shall be **apportioned among the several States** which may be included within this Union, **according to their respective numbers**, which shall be determined by adding to the whole number of free persons..."* [59]

Once the calculations have been made as to the federal taxes owed by the state's citizens to the federal government – the state now holding all tax monies required to be submitted by the state's affected citizenry, thus *indemnifying the citizen*, the State Treasurer would then assess the percentage of federal remittance due to fully fund any and all costs of programs associated with any federal mandate usually funded by the *return* of a state's federal tax dollars to the states by the federal government – mandates left unnullified – and *deduct* that amount to apply to the *state's* administration of said programs.

[59] https://www.archives.gov/founding-docs/constitution-transcript#1-9

Calculations would then be made to satisfy the state's original constitutionally mandated obligations, including our national obligation to the US military and its associated benefit programs as they relate to an apportionment of the state's population.

By the state intervening to co-opt the federal tax dollars that would come back to the state in the form of federal revenue streams for mandated programs, the state would not only be able to guarantee that all federally mandated programs left unnullified are fully funded and, therefore, available without pause. But it would also eliminate the federal government's ability to withhold those funds in an effort to "punish" a state for "bad behavior" (read: nullification).

As I stated before, much more learned minds than mine in the law (and specifically tax law) and the crafting of legislation and amendment proposals would need to be employed in this endeavor, but the basic premise is clear.

Regulating the remittance of federal taxes through the states achieves several goals:

- It prohibits the punishment of the states by the federal government via the withholding of federal funds necessary to fund mandated programs

- It starves the federal government into acquiescing to a budget

- It indemnifies each state from funding federal bailouts to other states or preferred private sector entities; it prevents the federal government from redistributing wealth from successful states to unsuccessful states

- Allows the states to titrate federal spending dollars to more judiciously fund programs within their state to the needs of the people

Further, because this move would effectively up-end the current unbalanced tax remittance scheme (the largest tax burden to the federal government and the smaller tax burden to the states would be up-ended to exist in the reverse) it goes without saying that the prospect of a larger revenue stream to the state would be attractive to every state legislator from every state.

And because Madison was correct when he said, "If men were angels, no government would be necessary. If angels were to govern men, neither external nor internal controls on government would be necessary," provisions should be included in any state legislation addressing the redirection of federal funds that establish mandated fiscal responsibility without the possibility of caveat at the state level.

ELIMINATING PUNISHMENT |
A RESTRUCTURING OF THE FEDERAL TAX SYSTEM

Another possibility in removing the federal government's ability to exact pain on states that employ nullification comes in a restructuring of the way we collect taxes from our citizens at both the federal and state levels.

A state could craft legislation that would – in part – create the aforementioned re-routing of federal tax dollar remittance but base that on an inversion of the way taxes are collected from the people. This inversion would result in the elimination of any form of tax on income and, instead, capitalize on one of the predominant strengths of our nation: consumption.

According to the Federal Reserve Bank of St. Louis, the United States is the leading consumer nation as of 2023 with an $18.526 trillion household final consumption expenditure standing at 69 percent of our nation's gross domestic product. This is $10 trillion more than the entirety of the European Union. We aren't just a consumer nation. We are *the* consumer nation.[60]

Inverting our current tax collection scheme from one based on income to one based on consumption would see tax collection happen – via algorithmic calculation upon a legislated percentage that addressed all of the aforementioned state-required deductions – in real-time at the moment of expenditure without the need for the citizenry to engage with the government regarding taxes at *any* time. Wherever a consumer exchange would take place – at any level of the product creative-market chain, the requisite taxes would be immediately deposited via ACH direct deposit to the state and federal treasuries.

[60] https://en.wikipedia.org/wiki/List_of_largest_consumer_markets#cite_note-3

In fact, legislation and/or a constitutional amendment could be codified to place each of these daily transactions on a blockchain, securing the remittance information permanently and transparently for anyone and everyone to examine on demand.

The inversion of our tax collection system would also remove the desire for the federally elected class to create "sweetheart deals" for their political benefactors. It would also greatly reduce the instances of corruption, cronyism, and the favoring of special interest agendas for two reasons, if not more:

1. The revenue coming into the federal government would be significantly reduced; there would exist no "slush fund" from which to derive money for pet projects or, what is commonly referred to as "pork"

2. The states would be withholding funding for the administration of federally mandated programs at the state level thus reducing the ability for lobbyists to be effective

There are several other positive aspects of employing a consumption tax to be noted here, although the purpose of this book is not to be an advocate for tax reform, *per se*. It is also honest to admit that there are some vulnerabilities to instituting a consumption tax, but using the several nations of the world that employ a consumption tax (also known in some nations as a value-added tax or VAT[61]) as models for how to legislate the institution of the vehicle devoid of pitfalls and using those models as a guide on what *not* to do, a consumption tax can be a vehicle that serves the people more fairly, holding government – at *all* levels – accountable.

Unlike a traditional income tax, which primarily targets individuals' earnings, a consumption tax focuses on what individuals and businesses *consume*. This introduces potential benefits for economic growth, sustainability, and – much to the glee of the spendthrifts in Washington and many state capitals, social welfare.

Perhaps the key advantage of a consumption tax lies in its simplicity and efficiency. Unlike income taxes, which require complex calculations, extensive documentation, and tax return filing, a consumption tax is relatively straightforward to implement and administer. This reduces the compliance burden – at both the federal and state levels – for both individuals and businesses, saving time, effort, and resources. Moreover, a consumption tax can be automated and integrated into point-of-sale systems, streamlining the collection process and significantly reducing the potential for tax evasion.

The institution of a consumption tax also incentivizes savings and investment, promoting long-term economic growth. By taxing consumption rather than income, individuals are encouraged to save a higher proportion of their income. This increased savings can be channeled

[61] https://www.investopedia.com/terms/v/valueaddedtax.asp

into investment, stimulating capital formation and fueling productive activities. In turn, this can lead to increased business expansion, job creation, and overall economic prosperity. As a result, a consumption tax can act as a catalyst for investment, contributing to a vibrant and dynamic economy.

A well-designed consumption tax system can also result in the enhancement of fairness and egalitarianism in taxation. Under an income tax regime, individuals with higher incomes may benefit from various deductions, exemptions, and loopholes, resulting in unequal tax burdens. In contrast, a consumption tax applies uniformly to *all* individuals, regardless of their income level. This ensures a more equitable distribution of the tax burden, as individuals with higher consumption patterns will pay a proportionately higher amount in taxes.

For example, if a billionaire decides that it is time for a new Gulfstream G650 private jet or a new Westport yacht, he or she would have to pay the applicable taxes on that purchase. By contrast, if a middle class American sought to purchase a used Jeep Wrangler, he or she would have to pay the applicable taxes on that purchase. The taxation is proportional and titrated to the ability to pay.

Furthermore, a consumption tax structure can be implemented, where essential goods and services – such as food, medicine and even housing costs – are taxed at lower rates or not taxed *at all*, shielding low-income households from excessive tax burdens.

The employment of a consumption tax also contributes to fiscal stability in that it provides a reliable source of revenue for governments, especially in the number-one consumer nation of the face of the earth: the United States.

Traditional income tax systems are often subject to fluctuations in economic cycles, leading to volatile revenue streams. In contrast, a consumption tax would lend itself to being much more stable, as it is based on consumption patterns, which are generally more consistent than income levels. This stability enables governments to better manage their expenditures while effectively broadening the tax base by capturing revenue from previously untaxed transactions, thereby increasing overall government revenue.

Even with the potential vulnerabilities that would come with inverting our tax system to one based on a consumption tax rather than an income tax, the benefits grossly outweigh the vulnerabilities, and the vulnerabilities could – as stated – be addressed in the wording of any codification and/or to the US Constitution.

Removing the federal government's ability to exact pain on the states is crucial to the success of this initiative. Without the ability to restrain the federal government's addiction to spendthrift financial policy, without a firewall to prevent a vindictive temper tantrum from the petulant child federal government this initiative would be an exercise in futility.

NULLIFICATION

REINVENTING GOVERNMENT: PARAMETERS TO NEUTER THE OPPORTUNISTS

"The several states composing the United States of America are not united on the principle of unlimited submission to their general government."

– Thomas Jefferson

In addition to establishing control over the federal government's penchant for encroaching on the sovereignty of states and trampling on the freedoms of Americans – not to mention its unbridled want to spend beyond its means, a longer vision plan that builds on the application of nullification and federal tax revenue re-routing comes in setting parameters for Congress.

While re-establishing how both houses of the Legislative Branch of the federal government work would require amending the US Constitution, that process, once state legislatures come to understand the power they have to affect federal change through the use of nullification, would become much more plausible.

And while the repeal of the 17th Amendment would free the American people from the smothering political capture of our governmental system and the drastic retooling of the 16th Amendment would benefit all concerned (less the spendthrifts of the federally elected class), several other "reformations" could be achieved that would serve to both make government, once again, the servant of the people and significantly damage the partisan hold that the political parties have on our federal government.

Among these reformations – and this is by no means a finite list to consider:

1. Limiting the length of legislative sessions
2. Implementing stand-alone legislation
3. Implementing term limits

4. Downsizing Government
5. Re-empowering the States

LIMITING THE LENGTH OF LEGISLATIVE SESSION
The current trend of the US Congress in its struggling to invent new ways to validate its existence has resulted in the incredible overreach of federal authority onto the sovereign state governments; sovereignty granted by the 9th and 10th Amendments to the US Constitution included in the Bill of Rights. One could argue this to be the case because there is an over-abundance of time spent in session allowing for free time to scheme said acquisition of power, unconstitutional as it is.

Currently, the US Constitution sets parameters for when Congress shall meet and stipulations on how and for how long each chamber may adjourn.

Article One, Section Four[62] states:

> *"The Congress shall assemble at least once in every Year, and such Meeting shall be on the first Monday in December, unless they shall by Law appoint a different Day…"*

And Article One, Section Five[63] states:

[62] https://www.archives.gov/founding-docs/constitution-transcript#1-4
[63] https://www.archives.gov/founding-docs/constitution-transcript#1-5

> *"Neither House, during the Session of Congress, shall, without the Consent of the other, adjourn for more than three days, nor to any other Place than that in which the two Houses shall be sitting."*

These entries in the Constitution place full control of when and for how long the US House of Representatives and the US Senate are in session in the hands of those who politically and opportunistically benefit from *being* in session.

But while it specifically stipulates that Congress "Shall assemble at least once each year," it does not mandate for *how long* Congress – as a whole – *must* remain in session.

A perfectly reasonable solution to establishing practical limitations for Congress is to limit the amount of time they are in session. This arrangement is not without precedent as it is currently applied in several states including in the State of Florida and the State of Texas.

In Florida, the official website of the Florida State Senate states:

> *"The Florida Legislature meets in session **every year for sixty consecutive days**. A regular session of the legislature shall convene on the first Tuesday after the first Monday in March of each odd-numbered year, and on the second Tuesday after the first Monday in January of each*

even-numbered year. There are other ways in which the Legislature may be convened as outlined in Article III, Section 3, of the Florida Constitution, including special sessions, which may be called either by the Governor; or by a joint proclamation issued by the Senate President and House Speaker. An extension of regular session or special session requires a three-fifths vote of each house." [64]

In Texas, the Texas House official website states:

*"The Legislature of the State of Texas, **operating under the biennial system**, convenes its regular sessions at noon on the second Tuesday in January of odd-numbered years. **The maximum duration of a regular session is 140 days**. The governor is given authority under the state constitution to convene the legislature at other times during the biennium. Such sessions are known as called or special sessions and are reserved for legislation that the governor deems critically important in the conduct of state affairs. Called sessions are limited to a period of 30 days, during which the legislature is permitted to pass laws only on subjects submitted by the governor in calling for the session."* [65]

---

[64] https://www.flsenate.gov/Session

[65]

https://www.house.texas.gov/resources/frequently-asked-questions/#how_leg

So, aside from special sessions that require an elevated threshold of need denoted by either the governors or the conglomeration of chamber leaders, both states – successful states by any measure and two states whose population grew in the chaotic time between 2020 and 2023 – have limited legislative sessions; compressed timetables during which elected officials *must* execute their duties to their constituents and the states.

The prolonged duration of legislative sessions of both the federal government and many state governments often leads to inefficiencies, partisan bickering, and legislative gridlock. Conversely, the benefits of limiting the duration of legislative sessions comes in a more focused and enhanced productivity, reduced costs, improved accountability, and increased public trust, the latter of which is in great need of repair.

By restricting, or compressing, the duration of legislative sessions, lawmakers are compelled to prioritize and address pressing issues in an expedited manner. Limited time-frames encourage legislators to streamline their efforts, leading to a more goal-oriented and targeted approach to policy making. The urgency to complete tasks within a limited and set period also discourages unnecessary delays while reducing political gamesmanship.

A shorter legislative session also necessitates more efficient decision-making processes. Time constraints discourage gratuitous and oftentimes meaningless partisan debate and encourage legislators to engage in substantive discussions, resulting in quicker resolutions based on honest compromise. This ensures that *essential* pieces of legislation are not subjected to prolonged delays or opportunistic filibustering tactics, enabling a more expeditious legislative process.

Additionally, limiting the duration of legislative sessions reduces the politically-generated scourge of legislative gridlock, where conflicting agendas and interests and partisan rivalries hinder progress. By placing time constraints on deliberations and the ability to complete legislative agendas, lawmakers are incentivized to find common ground and reach consensus more efficiently. This also fosters a more productive and cooperative legislative environment.

When considering what it costs to operate the federal and state legislatures it is only honest to admit that prolonged legislative sessions – such as are employed by the federal government and in states like Illinois, California, and New York, incur substantial costs in terms of operational expenses, including salaries, allowances, and administrative overhead. By imposing limitations on the length of legislative sessions, governments can significantly reduce these costs, relieving the burden on taxpayers' funds and allocating resources more judiciously. [66] [67] [68]

[66] https://www.ilga.gov/house/schedules/

[67] https://ballotpedia.org/2023_California_legislative_session

[68] https://indivisible.org/resource/indivisible-guide-new-york-state-legislature

Further, the uncertainty caused by prolonged legislative sessions can negatively impact economic stability and both national and local business environments. Limiting session durations provides clarity to businesses, investors, and citizens regarding the governmental direction of legislative activities. This necessarily creates more stability in decision-making processes fostering a more favorable economic climate that encourages investment and economic growth.

But, perhaps the most significant benefits of condensed and limited legislative sessions come in six areas:

1. Clearer Evaluation Metrics: Restricting the duration of legislative sessions enables a more accurate assessment of a lawmaker's performance, establishing a clear gauge to measure legislative productivity, responsiveness to constituents' needs, and the fulfillment of campaign promises. These metrics facilitate a more informed voting populace and that promotes both greater public engagement in the political and governmental process and greater accountability among elected officials.

2. Reduced Legislative Entrenchment: Lengthy legislative sessions can contribute to the entrenchment of certain lawmakers or political factions. By limiting the duration of legislative sessions, the political landscape becomes more dynamic, allowing for greater electoral turnover and increased competition among the political

class. Limiting the duration of legislative sessions aids in preventing complacency while promoting fresh perspectives and ideas within the legislative body.

3. Public Engagement & Oversight: A more restricted and condensed legislative session provides citizens with a more manageable time-frame to engage with their elected representatives; it allows for increased public participation, as constituents are more likely to actively follow and engage in legislative affairs. A limited session duration also enables more effective oversight by the media and civil society organizations, as well as the general public.

4. Restored Faith in Governmental Institutions: Public trust in governmental institutions is crucial for the stability and function of any society, yet today the level of trust bestowed upon our elected officials is almost less than zero. Limiting the duration of legislative sessions demonstrates a commitment to efficient governance and would serve as a starting point in the repair of the reputations of elected representatives.

5. Mitigating Political Fatigue: Unnecessarily lengthy legislative sessions can contribute to public disillusionment and political fatigue, as citizens witness prolonged partisan debates and little to no progress. By condensing the durations of legislative sessions, lawmakers are compelled to

be more committed to their principles and efficient, alleviating public frustration and fatigue associated with a seemingly unproductive and endless legislative process.

6. Increased Transparency: A more restricted legislative session promotes transparency in the policy-making process. By condensing the timeframe, legislators are more likely to engage in open debates, public consultations, and increased information sharing, helping citizens to better understand the legislative process. This, in turn, would help to restore trust and confidence in their elected representatives.

The potential gains in terms of governance efficiency, economic stability, transparency, and public confidence make the pursuit of limited legislative sessions a worthwhile endeavor.

INSTITUTING STAND-ALONE LEGISLATION

Stand-alone legislation refers to a legislative approach that focuses on addressing specific issues or concerns, as opposed to omnibus bills that encompass a wide range of unrelated provisions. The legislative action also mandates the *exclusion* of any unrelated amendments to the process which almost always facilitate gratuitous pork barrel spending and special interest earmarks.

The legislative process plays a crucial role in shaping the policies and regulations that govern the United States.

However, the sheer complexity and scope of contemporary governance often results in lengthy, convoluted, and non-consumable bills that address multiple unrelated issues simultaneously. This approach, commonly found in "omnibus" bills, can hinder transparency, accountability, and effective decision-making.

In contrast, stand-alone legislation offers a more focused and targeted approach, ensuring that specific concerns are addressed in a transparent, singular, and accountable manner.

Stand-alone legislation, also known as "single-issue legislation" or "single-subject legislation", aims to avoid the inclusion of unrelated provisions (read: pork and earmarks), promoting clarity and coherence in lawmaking. Stand-alone legislation can be enacted at various levels of government, including federal, state, or local levels, and can cover a wide range of subjects, such as individual budgets, entitlements, healthcare, environmental protection, or civil rights.

One of the primary benefits of stand-alone legislation is the improved transparency and accountability it brings to the legislative process. By focusing on specific issues, stand-alone legislation allows legislators, experts, and the public to more thoroughly scrutinize and better understand the proposed laws. This increased visibility facilitates robust debates, informed decision-making, and a higher level of legislative oversight.

Moreover, stand-alone legislation simplifies the task of tracking the progress and impact of specific laws, making it easier for citizens to hold their representatives accountable as each is on record for their singular vote on any specific subject. This eliminates the tired old and often used excuse by elected officials that they voted for or couldn't vote for a piece of legislation because of an amendment to the bill. It also eliminates the ability of disingenuous elected officials from *adding* amendments they know would damage or destroy any specific piece of legislation.

Unlike omnibus bills, which often contain unrelated provisions, stand-alone bills are less likely to be encumbered by unrelated debates or false-hearted political maneuvers. This streamlined process also reduces the likelihood of political horse-trading, where unrelated provisions are added to secure votes or to promote specific interests and/or support for other pieces of legislation, thus enhancing the overall integrity of the legislative process.

Because the implementation and enforcement of legislation can be challenging when bills encompass an overabundance of unrelated provisions, stand-alone legislation serves to simplify the implementation process, as the focus remains on a single issue or topic. Government agencies responsible for enforcing the law can, therefore, allocate their resources more efficiently, resulting in streamlined procedures and improved compliance rates.

Furthermore, stand-alone legislation facilitates the identification of potential gaps or shortcomings in the law, allowing for timely re-writes or adjustments to enhance effectiveness.

The focused nature of these bills also allow citizens, interest groups, and stakeholders to engage more meaningfully with specific issues that directly affect them. Public hearings, consultations, and open debates centered around the targeted issues in stand-alone bills encourage the active involvement of diverse perspectives, ensuring a more representative decision-making process. Consequently, stand-alone legislation goes to great lengths to promote public trust and legitimacy in governance.

When legislation addresses a single issue, it is easier for the public to comprehend and research the issue, as well as to engage with the proposed laws. Because stand-alone bills do not require an in-depth understanding of multiple complex topics, the entirety of the legislative process can be more accessible to citizens. This increased clarity enables citizens to become more aware of legislative developments and encourages them to actively participate in governmental processes. As a result, stand-alone legislation strengthens civic awareness and fosters a more informed and engaged citizenry.

One potential challenge associated with stand-alone legislation comes to us in the possibility of fragmented laws and regulations. Policymakers must carefully consider the potential impacts and broader implications when crafting stand-alone legislation to ensure comprehensive and harmonious governance. This lends itself to the argument that a *higher* intellectual level is appropriate for serving in public offices that are charged with crafting legislation.

Further, while stand-alone legislation is not immune to the influence of special interest groups and lobbying efforts, the targeted approach to the issue allows for the identification of individuals and groups who abuse the access lobbying affords deep-pocketed special interests. While focusing on a single issue may attract more attention from vested interests, leading to attempts to shape legislation to serve particular agendas, it is easier to identify, isolate and then take action against bad actors who don't have the best public interests at heart.

That said, policymakers and lawmakers must remain vigilant, transparent, and accountable to minimize the potential for undue influence and ensure that stand-alone legislation truly represents the interests and well-being of the broader population.

Because stand-alone legislation offers an over-abundance of benefits compared to its vulnerabilities, it serves as an excellent tool in providing fidelity to the constitutional limitations placed on the federal government.

INVOKING THE SPIRIT OF
GEORGE WASHINGTON IN TERM LIMITS

At the genesis of our Great American Experiment, we were fortunate to have Founders, Framers, and leaders who had fidelity to the notion that government should serve the people. This started, in earnest, with President George Washington's refusal to both accept coronation and to occupy office for more than two terms, an unwritten voluntary mandate that President Franklin D. Roosevelt arrogantly ignored in running for and then winning a third term. In his quest to fundamentally transform the United State government from one of service to one of spendthrift master, Roosevelt's third term served as the catalyst for the 22nd Amendment which reads:

> *"No person shall be elected to the office of the President more than twice, and no person who has held the office of President, or acted as President, for more than two years of a term to which some other person was elected President shall be elected to the office of the President more than once..."* [69]

The subject of term limits – constitutional or statutory provisions that restrict the number of times an individual can hold a particular elected office – are designed to facilitate a rotation of power and prevent the concentration of authority in the hands of an elite few

[69] https://www.archives.gov/founding-docs/amendments-11-27#xxii

individuals. And while term limits have been implemented in various democracies around the world, proving to bring numerous benefits, the federal government of the United States – that exists captured by the very political factions Washington warned of in his Farewell Address and whose average age as of 2023 stands at the third oldest in history – refuses to seriously entertain the governmental best practice.

Term limits play a crucial role in promoting accountability among elected officials, a common complaint leveled by the federal and several state governments by the American electorate. By imposing a limit on the number of terms an individual can serve, term limits create a sense of urgency and incentivize politicians to deliver results during their limited time in office. When politicians know they have a finite amount of time to enact policies and fulfill their promises, they are more likely to focus on the needs and aspirations of those who elected them. This heightened accountability ensures that elected officials remain responsive to the public's interests and act in the best interest of their constituents rather than those of the political benefactors and their own re-election prospects.

Limiting the number of terms someone can serve in any one governmental office offers a powerful tool in combating corruption within the political system. Prolonged incumbency – the longest-serving US Senator served 51 years[70] and the longest serving US

---

[70] https://www.senate.gov/senators/longest_serving_senators.htm

Representative having served 59 years[71] – can create an environment conducive to corruption, as politicians almost always become complacent, entrenched, or beholden to special interests. By limiting the number of terms an individual can serve, term limits disrupt the potential for long-term accumulation of power, reducing the opportunity for corruption while diminishing the influence of entrenched lobbying groups.

Term limits also significantly contribute to a healthy and vibrant democracy by encouraging a wider range of citizen participation. When elected offices have term limits, individuals from diverse backgrounds are more likely to step forward to seek public office. The absence of the advantage of incumbency levels the playing field and provides an opportunity for new candidates to challenge "establishment" politicians. This also encourages a wider pool of talent and ideas to enter politics, ensuring that the government is representative of the population it serves. Moreover, knowing that an elected position will become vacant because an office holder is term-limited motivates citizens to engage in the political process, fostering a more engaged and informed electorate.

Term limits also foster the realization of one of the ideological Left's favorite, unacted-upon buzzwords: diversity. Term limits help to promote political diversity by preventing the entrenchment of a single political party or

---

[71]

https://en.wikipedia.org/wiki/List_of_members_of_the_United_States_Congres s_by_longevity_of_service ideology in power. With limits on the number of terms an individual can serve, political power rotates among different individuals and parties over time. This rotation ensures that varying perspectives and ideologies are provided an opportunity to be represented in governance, preventing the domination of a single ideological or political group and reducing the likelihood of totalitarian authoritative tendencies. By promoting a healthy exchange of ideas and fostering a competitive political landscape, term limits would strengthen our Republic by encouraging compromise, collaboration, and consensus-building.

Lastly, but certainly not indicating the end of the list of the benefits of establishing term limits, they allow newly elected officials, unburdened by the constraints of incumbency, to propose innovative policies and challenges to the status quo. This influx of new voices injects dynamic energy into the political process, stimulating debate and ensuring that government remains responsive to the evolving needs of society.

Additionally, term limits prevent elected officials from becoming disconnected from the daily realities and concerns of the general population – including those they are tasked with representing, as they must step down and engage with constituents directly, fostering greater empathy and understanding.

DISMANTLING THE BUREAUCRACY BY ELIMINATING AGENCIES, DEPARTMENTS & COMMISSIONS

The benefits of downsizing the United States federal government while re-empowering the sovereignty of the states are numerous and significant. The current size and scope of the federal government have sparked debates about its effectiveness, efficiency, and impact on economic growth. The number of proponents to downsizing the federal government is growing. They argue that reducing the government's size and its involvement in various sectors can yield positive outcomes, such as improved efficiency, reduced bureaucracy, increased economic freedom, and enhanced accountability.

The US federal government's size and scope have grown significantly over time. This expansion has led to accusations of unconstitutional overreach and concerns about the potential infringement on individual freedoms and state autonomy, both of which I will address here.

One of the primary arguments for downsizing the federal government is the potential for improved efficiency and effectiveness. Advocates argue that a leaner government structure would be better equipped to respond to challenges, make faster decisions, and allocate resources more efficiently and that downsizing leads to a reduction in bureaucracy and the elimination of redundant or unnecessary regulations and processes resulting in faster and more responsive government.

Another point of contention is that by reducing the government's role in the economy, downsizing can foster economic freedom and the stimulation of innovation. Advocates argue that fewer regulations and interventions allow free market forces to operate more liberally, leading to increased entrepreneurship, competition, and economic growth.

Another point that the proponents for the downsizing of the federal government make is that it facilitates enhanced accountability and responsiveness. Downsizing can promote greater accountability by simplifying decision-making processes and reducing layers of bureaucracy. This can result in clearer lines of responsibility and improved public oversight, ultimately enhancing the government's responsiveness to citizens' needs.

So, now that the argument for downsizing the size and scope of the federal government – or at least several key points of argument – has been established, our focus needs to spotlight downsizing strategies and approaches

One approach to downsizing is to consolidate or eliminate federal agencies that have overlapping functions or duplicative efforts, both at the federal and at the state levels. Almost every state has agencies that render their federal counterparts redundant, bureaucratic, and in many cases oppressively ideological.

A great example of this comes in both the Environmental Protection Agency and the US Department of Education.

Every state has its own version of the EPA and every state has a department charged with providing oversight to the individual school governing bodies, the latter of which exists as a redundancy on the state level. By streamlining the organizational structure to eliminate the federal EPA and Department of Education, the government can not only return proper authority to the states, but it can also reduce federal administrative costs, eliminate redundancy, and improve coordination among necessary agencies.[72]

The elimination of redundant governance at the federal level can also simplify regulations and processes, reducing the burden on businesses and individuals while making compliance easier and less costly. This – in and of itself – can stimulate economic growth, encourage innovation, and improve the overall efficiency of government operations.

A downsizing of the federal government in the elimination of redundancy also promotes decentralized decision-making. Decentralizing decision-making processes not only moves our Republic away from centralized governance – which our Framers abhorred, but it empowers local authorities and communities to address their own specific needs and priorities. It can lead to more effective, appropriate, tailored, and effective solutions, as decisions are made by those who have a superior understanding of local dynamics and challenges.

[72] https://en.wikipedia.org/wiki/List_of_federal_agencies_in_the_United_States

The downsizing of the federal government can also create opportunities for increased collaboration between the public and private sectors but at a manageable local level avoiding the temptation of leaning toward a textbook action of fascism. Local public-private partnerships can leverage the strengths of both sectors, leading to innovative solutions, cost savings, and improved service delivery, and serving as a petri dish for solutions that can be crafted at a federal level; solutions that protect the free market and the rights of the citizenry.

There are several case studies of success where the notion of downsizing a nation's government is concerned:

1. The United Kingdom: The United Kingdom embarked on an extensive downsizing effort in the 1980s and 1990s. The reforms included privatization of state-owned enterprises, reduction of government regulations, and restructuring of public services. These measures resulted in improved efficiency, reduced bureaucracy, and enhanced economic growth.

2. New Zealand: New Zealand implemented significant downsizing reforms in the 1980s and 1990s, including deregulation, privatization, and decentralization. The country experienced increased economic freedom, improved fiscal discipline, and enhanced competitiveness as a result.

3. Sweden: Sweden initiated a series of reforms in the 1990s to downsize its public sector and reduce the government's involvement in the economy. The measures included tax reductions, deregulation, and the introduction of market-oriented reforms. Sweden's downsizing efforts led to increased economic growth and improved fiscal stability.

4. Canada: In the 1990s, Canada implemented a downsizing strategy to address its fiscal challenges. The reforms included reducing the size of the federal government, cutting public spending, and implementing fiscal discipline measures. Canada's downsizing efforts resulted in improved fiscal health, increased efficiency, and sustained economic growth, that is until the Trudeau era.

Downsizing the US federal government will not be without challenges. There will inevitably be an enormous amount of resistance from special interests, the gratuitous elected class, and other vested interests who will support bureaucratic inertia and politically motivated obstacles. Overcoming these challenges; defanging the swamp creatures of the establishment status quo in Washington, DC, will require effective leadership at the state level, strong public engagement, and a clear vision for the future.

Approaching the dismantling and downsizing of the US federal bureaucracy requires a careful approach to ensure that essential services and programs are successfully transitioned to the state and more local levels. It will be crucial to prioritize core functions and identify areas where downsizing can be implemented without adversely affecting critical services, a degradation which would result in the loss of support for the decentralization of federal power.

In executing a decentralization and downsizing of the federal bureaucracy, a comprehensive plan including input from citizens, businesses, and select experts, can help ensure that the downsizing efforts align with the needs and aspirations of the preservation of the Republic.

Effective communication is critical to gaining public support and addressing concerns about the decentralization of the federal government. Transparent communication about the benefits, challenges, and progress of the downsizing process can help manage public perception and build trust in the effort.

Once the truth that the government closest to the people is the more responsive and effective government is realized, and that a transition from centralized government and the re-empowerment of state governments will better serve the people, support for the action will grow and the fear-tactics the federal government uses to keep the population in subservience will fade.

RE-EMPOWERING THE STATES
TO CONSTITUTIONALITY

In the United States, the relationship between state and federal governments has been a subject of ongoing debate since the country's inception. While both levels of government have their merits, the federal government exists guilty of encroaching on the relationship in contradiction to the limitations placed upon it by the US Constitution.

This fact – and it is a fact, mandates the serious consideration of the subject of this book: Nullification.

Appropriately empowered state governments offer numerous advantages over a more powerful federal government. Enhanced and more potent representation, policy responsiveness, experimentation, local autonomy, and the preservation of ideological and political diversity are all critical aspects that contribute to effective governance and a thriving Republic.

By empowering state governments – and doing so through the embrace of nullification at the state level, we can foster a more inclusive and participatory system that better serves the diverse needs and aspirations of our nation's citizens

State governments, by nature, are closer in authoritative proximity to their constituents than the federal government. This proximity allows state officials to better understand and address the specific needs, values, and priorities of their local communities. This is the argument behind the block granting of federal funds to the states for the *states* to administer. Further, state politicians are more likely to directly interact with their constituents, developing a stronger sense of responsibility towards them.

State governments are infinitely better suited to appropriately prioritize and tailor policies to meet the unique requirements of their citizens. There is a high probability that what is appropriate for the citizens of New York, Illinois, and California is highly inappropriate for the citizens of Idaho, South Dakota, and South Carolina. States can also address regional disparities and implement localized solutions resulting in a more effective resolution to local issues. And a more powerful state government presents a higher likelihood of policies aligning with the cultural, economic, and social characteristics of the state's population.

The re-institution of stronger state governments empowers citizens by providing more opportunities for direct participation. With fewer layers of government between the people and their representatives, individuals have increased access to the decision-making process and a greater ability to shape policies that directly affect them.

State governments also have the power to respond more swiftly to emerging challenges and changing circumstances due to their smaller size and streamlined decision-making processes. A great example of this comes in disaster response.

For example, in 2022, Florida Governor Ron DeSantis was able to swiftly and effectively mitigate a response to Hurricane Ian. Rather than wait for the President and FEMA officials to react through the ribbons of bureaucratic federal red tape, DeSantis called on the power of Florida's state government, in coordination with a great many county governments, to execute one of the most timely and effective responses to a hurricane-induced disaster the state has ever experienced.

The State of Florida adjusted policies to meet the evolving needs of its residents without waiting for federal action, ensuring a more prompt and effective response to the disaster and the many challenges created in its aftermath.

A more powerful state government allows for greater policy experimentation, allowing for true innovation and variety in governance approaches to individual issues. States – as the Framers of the US Constitution held – can serve as laboratories for new ideas, policies, and programs, testing their viability and effectiveness before broader implementation into the world of the federal government.

Again, a great example of this comes in the diverse responses to the COVID pandemic by several states – including Florida, Texas, and South Dakota – that refused to fall prey to what we now know was a false-narrative stressing quarantine of the total of populations, masking, and mass vaccination. In the end, the policies developed at the state levels in Florida, Texas, and South Dakota proved more effective than the draconian and incorrect guidance/mandates coming out of the federal government and its bureaucratic agencies and departments..

The flexibility afforded Florida, Texas, and South Dakota – as well as others, enabled these states to find localized solutions to the complex problem while encouraging a healthy approach to the issues to the benefit of their citizens.

Individual state governments possess a deeper understanding of their local economies, industries, and environmental factors, knowledge most often overlooked by the overreaching federal government. With greater autonomy, state governments can adopt regulations that *best* suit their unique circumstances, promoting sustainable economic growth and safeguarding and serving the well-being of their citizens.

Additionally, a more powerful state government upholds the principle of subsidiarity, which advocates for decisions to be made at the lowest competent level of governance. By devolving power to states, the federal government acknowledges the importance of local autonomy and diversity, preserving the values and traditions that are crucial to our Republic's social fabric, unique fabrics that the global elite seek to homogenize into oblivion.

The United States is a diverse nation, comprised or different regions with distinct cultural, social, and historical backgrounds. While activist special interest groups seek to erase those distinct cultural flavors, individualisms, and histories, to deny these facts is to deny who we are as a people; it flies in the face of our legacy: *e pluribus unum*.

A more powerful and sovereign state government recognizes and respects this cultural and historical diversity, allowing states to maintain and celebrate their unique identities. State autonomy also safeguards the rights and values of minority groups and indigenous groups ensuring their voices are heard in decision-making processes.

Further, re-empowering state governments to the level of constitutionality would act as a check against federal government overreach. It would provide safeguards against the concentration of power and prevent a single entity from making decisions that may or may not be in the best interest of every state or region.

State governments can protect their citizens' rights and interests by asserting their independence, doing so through the employment of nullification when necessary, striking the right balance between state and federal power and ensuring that the United States remains a beacon of freedom, responsive to the unique circumstances of its people.

NULLIFICATION

CONCLUSION:
IT CAN WORK IF WE WORK SMART

"Most of the things worth doing in the world had been declared impossible before they were done."

– Louis D. Brandeis

To be sure, the effort it will take to achieve the successful use of nullification – an effort to bring about the change our Republic so desperately needs to get back to our constitutional roots – will be significant and akin to a state codifying a new amendment to the US Constitution.

The important difference here is that the effort would, in and of itself, be a positive step toward the use of nullification because the members of the codifying state legislatures would realize the benefits of using the procedure and be cohesive in the understanding of when and how to use the legislative tool.

Another positive aspect of a state adopting the use of nullification and its associated reforms is that upon the adoption comes to us the reality that its use can take effect without the additional codification of other states. Upon adoption, each state – unlike the Convention of States movement (which I endorse) – can codify and enact the use of nullification individually. As each state begins the process of using nullification, re-crafting its revenue schemes, and overruling redundant federal agencies, departments, and commissions, other states will witness the benefits in real-time. Participating states would exist as argument models for other states.

Further, with each state's adoption of nullification, the decentralization of the federal government becomes an increasing reality, which reduces the threat posed to our Republic by opportunistic special interests and ideological change agents.

On June 7th, 2023, the State of Louisiana codified into law their right to embrace nullification as a legal and legitimate tool in the face of unconstitutional overreach by the federal government.

Louisiana State Senator Stewart Cathey (R-33), introduced Joint Concurrent Resolution SCR21[73], a simply stated four page document referencing Louisiana's State Constitution, stating, in part:

> *"...Be it resolved that the Legislature of Louisiana does hereby affirm the sovereign right of Louisiana to nullify unconstitutional acts of the federal government."*

Although this piece of codified legislation doesn't protect the State of Louisiana from acts of retribution by a coercive federal government, it serves as the basis for constitutionally based action by a sovereign state to push back against the continued encroachment by the federal government into state sovereignty.

As stated previously, the dangers associated with the current scheme being employed by our federal government, a scheme to achieve centralized government, are quite real. We as a nation and as citizens of the fifty sovereign states are already witnessing the concentration of power into the hands of the privileged class in the two major national political

[73] https://www.legis.la.gov/Legis/ViewDocument.aspx?d=1331621

parties and the elitist assembly of chosen few that count themselves among the inner-circles in the halls of power.

We are affected by the erosion of democratic principles to the point that the Executive Branch suffers no consequences for their rule by Executive Order, many times executed with the full knowledge that the actions they are executing are unconstitutional. A perfect example of this comes to us in the Biden administration's now-struck student loan forgiveness program. This blatant redistribution of wealth – until ruled unconstitutional by the US Supreme Court in June of 2023 – had no legal, moral, or ethical footing in serving the "common good". Instead, it was a blatant raiding of the federal treasury; a blatant and opportunistic use of taxpayer dollars to benefit a political re-election campaign.

And the dangers of centralized government don't begin and end with the unconstitutional use of Executive Orders. Because our federal government has morphed from being one that serves the people (representative government) to one built on the arrogance of elitism, academia, and public-private enterprise (neo-fascism), special interests exist tunnel-visioned in their quest to more deeply capture the halls of the federal bureaucracy, even as the purveyors of transformation continue their subjugation of our society.

Where in the 1970s and 1980s political correctness was consumed as an amusement, today the Marxist-based woke movement has traveled on the coattails of political correctness to exist as an ingrained and advancing influence of totalitarianism in our culture and in our halls of power.

Where many on both the Right and the Left of our contemporary political spectrum ascribe to the false notion that wokeism is a product of American and Western enlightenment (approximately 60 percent of those who identify at Democrats believe being woke is a "good thing"), the movement's genesis is parked *squarely* in the anarchism that facilitated the genesis of Marxism and, through that, the same consequential mentality that fomented Mao's "cultural revolution", which resulted in the genocidal slaughter of over 80 million human beings.

As Ginsburg-Milstein fellow AJ Caschetta, a principal lecturer at the Rochester Institute of Technology, wrote[74]:

> *"...the political metaphor of sleeping and waking was at the core of the pre-revolutionary Russian propaganda disseminated by the self-described terrorist group, Narodnaya Volya (People's Will). The origins of what many now call the 'Great Awokening' can be plainly seen in the ideas of a handful of thinkers who developed and directed what historian David C. Rapoport calls the first wave of modern terrorism: the Anarchist wave.*

[74] https://spectator.org/the-anarchists-roots-of-wokeism/

"The parallels between early European socialism (1840-1880) and today are numerous. Dissatisfied with capitalism, agitators sought to convince the people to rise up and overthrow governments and the privileged classes who supported them. But they were frustrated with their inability to persuade the masses who were unaware of their oppression. The agitators were ambivalent towards the masses, recognizing that they needed 'the people' for their revolution but also hating them for not having already joined the revolution of their own volition. John Most, the German anarchist exiled to France, then England, then America, described them as 'swells and other fat-faced philistines…happy in this stage of unfreedom as pigs in muck.'

"People needed to be convinced that their lives were miserable, and too many of them, the anarchists believed, were blissfully unaware of their plight. So the metaphor was born: the people are sleeping fools in need of an awakening.

"This is the same metaphor at the heart of wokeism…"

Even an elementary examination of the evolution of Marxism reveals the obvious parallels between the activists of the initial anarchist wave of the fledgling Marxists into the West and the opportunistic elements in their pursuit of fundamental transformation today.

Consider these turn of the 19th Century points held by the early European socialist movement circa 1840-1880, as denoted by Caschetta:

1. The anarchists believed that people would wake up and listen if they were shown that the morality of their *system was corrupt*; that they had been *victimized*

2. Since traditional propaganda had failed, they came up with "propaganda by deed," (read: "direct action") and the deeds were, by necessity, executed through *violence*

3. Anarchists formed "vanguard groups," designed to lead by example and wake the people from their sleep (read: groups like Antifa and BLM)

Each of these common points can be found in the movements of both the anarchists of the late 1800s and the more contemporary crop of woke activists executing their 20th- and 21st-century brand of anarchism; anarchism that champions the fundamental transformation of the United States of America from a Constitutional Republic to a country kneeling to democratic socialism and then full-blown communist Marxism.

According to the executive summary of an article titled, *Far-Left Extremist Groups in the United States*[75], published by the Counter Extremist Project:

> *"The far-Left encompasses multiple ideologies, but security experts believe that a large percentage of far-Left radicals subscribe to at least one of three main classifications: anarchism, communism/socialism/Marxism, and autonomous radicals. Far-left groups have largely embraced social justice as a raison d'être in protest of perceived restrictions on liberty by the state. In the early and mid-20th century, the Communist Party USA (CPUSA) played a subversive role in promoting communism in the United States and aligned itself with the Soviet Union. Today, CPUSA promotes...communism...as the only guarantor of those freedoms..."*

Historically – and to put the dangers of centralized government into bone-chilling context, the world's most egregious acts of societal and cultural genocide rests solely with governments whose despotic dictators embraced one form of centralized government or another, i.e. communism, socialism, Marxism, and Maoism. The body count[76] attributed to these "isms" is sickeningly stunning:

[75] https://www.counterextremism.com/content/far-left-extremist-groups-united-states

[76] https://en.wikipedia.org/wiki/List_of_genocides

- Mao's Cultural Revolution (1966-1976) – Launched by Mao Zedong, its stated goal was to preserve Chinese communism by purging remnants of capitalist and traditional elements from Chinese society to the tune of over 20,000,000 killed, with some scholars[77] estimating up to 80,000,000 killed.

- Stalin's Russian Revolution (1917-1923) – Between the Red Terror, the White Terror, and the Bolshevik Revolution, the body count that resulted in Josef Stalin's reign of totalitarian oppression in the Soviet Union numbered over 61,000,000

- The Holocaust (1941-1945) – Under Adolf Hitler and the Nazi SS, over 7,000,000 people including Christians, Gypsies, homosexuals, and over two-thirds of the Jewish population in Europe were slaughtered.

- Holodomor (1932-1933) – A purposely manufactured famine in Soviet Ukraine that killed over 5,000,000 Ukrainians.

- Generalplan Ost (1939-1945) – The government of Nazi Germany's plan for the genocide and ethnic cleansing and colonization of Central and Eastern Europe by Germans saw the

[77] https://www.washingtonpost.com/archive/politics/1994/07/17/how-many-died-new-evidence-suggests-far-higher-numbers-for-the-victims-of-mao-zedongs-era/01044df5-03dd-49f4-a453-a033c5287bce/

extermination of over 3,000,000 people including approximately 10 percent of the total Polish gentile population.

- Cambodian Genocide (1975-1979) – The systematic persecution and killing of over 3,000,000 Cambodian citizens by the Khmer Rouge under the leadership of Communist Party of Kampuchea general secretary Pol Pot

While many give little weight to the idea of atrocities like these happening in the United States, it cannot be denied that would someone have asked a citizen of the Soviet Union in 1980 if they thought their country would cease to exist at the turn of the 21st century the response would have been a resounding rebuke of the notion. But, to that same Soviet citizen, the turn of the century delivered a very different reality.

The dangers – the *mortal* dangers – of unbridled and unchecked centralized government stand historically verifiable and make a serious and potent argument for the pre-emptive decentralization of the US federal government, especially given their support for the transformative powers of the woke movement, a movement anchored in Marxism.

Additionally, today in the United States, we have a federal government, federal bureaucratic apparatus, and an assembly of elitists and globalists who collude with the aforementioned to both exist as an oligarchic public-private federal government but also to glean opportunity and fortune off the backs of the American taxpayers.

As I write this, the national debt of the United States of America stands at $32 trillion[78] and rising at a frighteningly rapid pace. Even so, the federal government – both the Legislative Branch and the Executive Branch, during times of control by both national political parties – continues to spend grotesquely beyond the means of what the American taxpayer can afford.

We exist (and these figures continue to rise at an alarming rate) $1.1 trillion in debt to Japan, $859 billion in debt to Communist China, $668 billion in debt to the United Kingdom, $331 billion in debt to Belgium, and $318 billion in debt to Luxembourg. This is on top of the $24.6 trillion owed in public debt and other financial obligations that total our current debt at the $32 trillion figure, as of this writing.

Yet each administration in the 21st century – regardless of whether the seats of power were held by Republicans or Democrats – has left the next administration and future generations of Americans saddled with debt that, realistically, can *never* be repaid.

Since 2000, each administration in power has added to the debt[79] in dramatic and alarming ways:

---

[78] https://www.usdebtclock.org/

[79] https://www.investopedia.com/us-debt-by-president-dollar-and-percentage-7371225

- Joe Biden[80] – $2,499,993,043,258.10 (first year)
- Donald Trump – $6,700,491,178,561.60
- Barack Obama – $7,663,615,710,425.00
- George W. Bush – $4,217,261,484,712.34

The fact that this egregious fiscal irresponsibility at the federal level has been perpetrated by *both* political parties – even as each and every politician running for office feigns concern about out national debt, yet does nothing once elected to stop deficit spending – proves beyond any argument that the federally elected class is incapable of budgeting within the means of our revenue streams.

That no officially legislated budget has been codified since 2014[81] serves as proof positive that the finances of the United States are nothing more than a re-election issue for those elected to federal office.

So, the obvious indictment of our federal government to warrant decentralizing the institution exists quite starkly:

- We cannot trust our federally elected officials to accurately represent the citizenry

- We cannot trust our federal government to be good stewards of our tax dollars

---

[80] https://www.self.inc/info/us-debt-by-president/

[81] https://www.theguardian.com/world/2014/jan/17/congress-finally-passes-us-budget

- We cannot trust the special-interest-held federally elected class to keep the best interests of their constituencies held above their own personal and financial interests

- We cannot trust our federally elected officials to jealously execute fidelity to both the United States Constitution and the sovereignty of our Republic

- And we cannot trust the federal government – including all of its bureaucratic departments, agencies, commissions, and other sycophantic entities – to maintain its allegiance to the very principles that were used to create our Republic; to individualism, the inalienable rights to "Life, Liberty, the Pursuit of Happiness", and equal opportunity for all. We cannot trust them to have fealty to Americanism.

The enactment of nullification at the state level, the re-crafting of revenue schemes to effect fiscally responsible and controlled remittance to the federal government in a manner that neuters its ability to punish states for ideological and/or political reasons, and the beginning of the process that allows states to negate regulatory edicts from redundant federal agencies, departments, and commissions all while countermanding unconstitutional mandates by an overreaching and agendized federal government, will result in an immediate realization of benefits, both financially and culturally.

Although the fight to achieve these solutions will be a hard one, in the end, the re-institution of the sovereignty of states to their original authority under the Constitution and Bill of Rights – the authority our Framers *intended* for the states and for us will, without doubt, serve to avoid the metastasizing of an irreversible march toward "dis-union". In the end, the invoking of nullification and the required measures to support its potency will allow us to pass a healthier Republic on to future generations.

Let's hope we are wise enough – at *state* levels – to do what is right for our Republic, its people, and – *hopefully* – its future generations.

May God bless the United States of America.

ABOUT THE AUTHOR

Frank Salvato is the Vice President of News & Information Operations for GEMCOM, a Division of LimComm, LLC, and the CEO of The CompassPoint Group. He is the publisher and host of the Underground USA[82] read on a dedicated Substack platform; the podcast heard on iHeart Radio, Pandora, Spotify, Amazon Podcasts, and anywhere podcasts are heard.

Salvato served as the Executive Director at BasicsProject a grassroots, non-partisan, research and education initiative focusing on Constitutional Literacy, and internal and external threats facing Western Civilization including threats posed by Islamofascism and the Marxist-based American Fifth Column. His organization, BasicsProject, partnered in producing the original national symposium series addressing the root causes of Islamofascist terrorism.

His analysis has been recognized by the US House International Relations Committee and the Japan Center for Conflict Prevention, and his opinion and analysis have been published by The American Enterprise Institute, The Washington Times, The Jewish World Review, Accuracy in Media, Human Events, Breitbart.com, and Townhall.com, and are syndicated nationally.

---

[82] https://www.undergroundusa.com/

Salvato has been a featured guest on al Jazeera's *Listening Post*, Radio Belgrade One, and ITN's *Truthloader* Program in the UK. He appeared on *The O'Reilly Factor* on FOX News Channel, and was featured in the documentary, *Ezekiel and the MidEast 'Piece' Process: Israel's Neighbor States*.

He is the author of six monographs examining Islamofascism and Progressivism, including "Understanding the Threat of Radical Islam", "Women in the Fundamentalist Islamic Culture", and "The United States of America Is Not a Democracy".

He can be heard twice weekly on "The Captain's America: Third Watch" radio program syndicated nationally on the USA Radio, Salem, and Genesis Communication Networks.

NOTES

NOTES

NOTES